The Blueprint for a Successful Practice

Methods of Marketing Your Business & Increasing Your Bottom Line

Gina L. Spielman, LCSW, C.H.

Table of Contents

If you can imagine it, you can achieve it; if you can dream it, you can become it.

~ William Arthur Ward

Acknowledgements

As you all know, most books are not written without the contribution of others or the experience of working with them. So, I would first like to thank my wonderful husband, Eric, who has provided me with an incredible amount of support, encouragement, and ideas. With his sharp intelligence, natural willingness to help, and his management and business education, we make a great team. I would also like to thank all of the counselors that have worked in my practice as well as all of my consultation clients who have allowed me to work with them in order to build their practices. I have had the privilege to work with so many nice people and all of those experiences have helped me tremendously in writing this book. I would also like to thank my parents for instilling in me sound money management skills and responsibility, which has laid the groundwork for writing this book. Last but not least, I would like to thank my mentor, Eileen Cole, LCSW, who has also helped spark ideas and provided much encouragement and support as well. Without all of these people, this book would not have been possible.

Foreword

Congratulations on your decision to build your practice! Since you are reading this book, I am assuming you have decided to grow your business. I wish you well on the start of your exciting business-building journey!

This book comes from a "psychotherapy and hypnosis" practice perspective, because that is my specialty, but there will be many suggestions and bits of advice that can be used in all healthcare, healing, and private practice settings, even in general business as well. So, if you own a business, I am confident this book will be useful to you. Please note that I will use the word "client" many times, as that is what we call the people who utilize the services in my practice. You may substitute the word "client" for "patient", "customer", "account", and so forth, in most situations while reading this book, depending on your type of business.

This book does not contain extravagant or complicated philosophies because I believe in a "nuts and bolts" approach to growing and maintaining a business. This book contains "no fluff" and is realistic, direct, and easy to follow. You will not find many "exercises" because I believe in a "just do it" approach and that most of the necessary activities will be the marketing methods themselves. I believe that if you spend the time just doing the methods and following the advice, then you will see results. Confidence and self-actualization are sure to follow.

At this point, I would like you to ask yourself some questions about your current or future practice. Do you have too few clients and too much time on your hands? Or are you spending too much time for too little money? Are you unsure where to spend your marketing time or dollars? Possibly you are having trouble getting paid for your services or feel like you are not keeping enough of what you earn. Maybe you would you like to get more referrals and keep them coming back for more. Would you like training on how to "make the sale" when you have a potential client or referral source on the line? Or perhaps you would like to learn how to attract a certain type of clientele into your caseload. Maybe you just need some support, validation and encouragement through your practice-building experience. If your response was "yes" to any of the above statements, then this book is sure to help.

Having solid clinical knowledge and skills, and connecting well with clients, may be sufficient for providing good services. However, it will not attract enough clients to build a practice. Receiving referrals on a continual basis is necessary for building a successful practice. Diversifying your referral sources is key to your continued growth. However, this is where many professionals struggle. Many therapists feel awkward about business and marketing, they may dread it, or may not know what to do or how to do it. I don't know about you, but I cannot remember a single course in school that taught anything about owning a business or marketing a practice. However, after reading this book, you will have "the blueprint" to grow your business. Marketing really is simply creating a desired product or service and then getting the word out about that product or service. It is just the "how", "where", "what", and knowing how to pay the lowest cost for the most referrals, which this book will fully touch upon. I have had to learn from experience, by discussing with other professionals and observing what they were doing, by trial and error on some methods, and reading anything I could get my hands on. I found some very surprising things during my journey. Two of the most surprising discoveries were that you do not have to be an extravert to market your practice well, and you do <u>not</u> need to have much money! My practice receives multiple referrals most business days and I want to teach you how you can do the same with your practice!

It is important to diversify your business by developing a large number of referral sources as well as a few different "income streams" (psychotherapy, writing, consulting, teaching, and so forth). Diversification increases the chances you can create significant income ongoing, and it can be rewarding in other ways as well, such as making your work more interesting. In my practice, we have set up countless referral sources as well as a few different "income streams", so if one dries up, we will all be fine. This book will frequently touch upon how to diversify as well as create other sources of income.

Today's marketplace is complex. I am sure you have worried a great deal about building and maintaining a private practice. I know how it is. On one side, you have managed care that seems to be involved in an increasing amount of cases. Then you have the economic downturn which is affecting countless clients and their ability or willingness to pay for services. In addition, there seems to be fierce competition in some areas. I know at times it may seem a bit hopeless. However, this book will give several methods which will allow your practice to co-exist with managed care companies, provide direct "to the point" recommendations that can "recession-proof" your practice, and offer sound advice on how to stand out in a crowd over other professionals.

A LITTLE ABOUT ME

Here is a bit of personal information to help you get a feel for where my perspectives originate. All of my schooling and professional life has been in Illinois, some in rural areas, but mostly in the Chicago metropolitan area. I attended Southern Illinois University, where I received a BA in Psychology, and then attended University of Illinois-Chicago where I earned a Master's Degree. I am a Licensed Clinical Social Worker and a Certified Hypnotist. For the past 13 years, I have been providing psychotherapy as well as managing my private practice. At the time of writing this book, I currently have two counseling offices. One is in Naperville, Illinois, which would be considered a typical Chicago suburb, with an urban feel. My second office is in Oswego, Illinois, which is more of a small-town atmosphere. I have also worked many years in national Employee Assistance Programs (EAPs) as well as in managed care settings.

Having a proven track record of building up a successful group practice, I have countless "tried and true" suggestions and recommendations. I have also learned the hard way with various methods and will share those as well, as I think that information is invaluable. I decided to write this book after realizing I had volumes of useful information from all the years of working as a professional, as well as everything I have learned from building a practice. In general, other professionals seem to be unaware of several ways they can market themselves free or low cost, as well as other tips on how to increase income. They frequently try to "pick my brain" to find out how a practice can receive so many referrals. Often, they seem to be in need of information on the "ins and outs" of insurance and EAP companies. Also, I have realized I may think a bit differently than most other therapists, seeing ways that they may not see, in regards to practice-building, marketing, and increasing income. With my practice, when all of the counselors began to have schedules full of clients, I found myself not having to use the information and skills (in practice-building) anymore. I had to do something to keep my passion alive, so I started a consulting service for other professionals on how to build their practices, and then started the book! I hope that you will take full advantage of this book for you and your current or future practice.

Success is the sum of small efforts, repeated day in and day out.

~ Robert Collier

Chapter One

Where to Spend Your Marketing Time and Dollars

Marketing in private practice is simply producing desired services and then getting the word out about those services. I assume you have already completed the major part of your schooling. The good news is that your completed schooling is the most difficult part of creating a desired service. Now let us put the finishing touches on that to create more of what the public just has to have, and then work on getting that information out to as many people as possible. As mentioned earlier, what is surprising about all of this is that you do not need to be a marketing professional or have an extravert personality to market your practice well. You also do not need to have a fortune. In fact, I myself am an introvert personality type, have no formal marketing training, and began my practice with very little money. Currently I am usually getting multiple referrals per business day into my practice, and bringing a considerable amount of revenue into my business.

mber, you are selling the "experience" of therapy if you are a mental health professional, and you are selling a connection with you as well as your credentials, expertise, and abilities. So, whenever a potential client might get more of a picture of how her counseling experience would be with you, the better. So, whatever you can do to get those messages across, the better. Keep this in mind while marketing, as it will help.

Also keep in mind that people like passion. People like feeling that they are putting themselves and their family into the hands of someone who really loves what he or she is doing. I suppose it is because we know, from human nature, that if people love their job, they will most likely put more effort and care into their work. So let your passion show! Last but not least, when using the marketing methods in this chapter, always remember there is great need for your services out there, which can help you stay motivated!

In working on these marketing methods, you will also want to consistently keep in mind the concept of diversification and how that can be an "insurance plan" for your practice. In the past, I was working with another social worker at a managed care company, and he said he was working there because he had to close his practice. One of the main reasons that he had to close it was because his "referral source" had dried up. Apparently, his main contract was an HMO, and all of the sudden, he lost all of those referrals. I am not sure if the service contract just changed (which happens frequently with services and insurance companies), or if they decided they did not want to refer to him anymore. Anyhow, the result was the same. Well, this stayed in my mind for all these years and has drilled into me the extreme importance of diversifying. You will need to diversify, particularly in the "referral sources" realm, but also in the "income streams" and "additional services" areas of your business, in order to grow and sustain your income. You will want the peace of mind that comes with knowing that a referral source or certain "income stream" can dry up without affecting the bottom line of your business.

You will find almost all of the methods here to be quite easy to use, in addition to being free or very low cost. Nonetheless, there needs to be a well-rounded and diverse plan of action. If your goal is to be in full-time private practice relatively quickly, then I suggest you work full-time hours building your practice until you actually reach your goal. So, during that time, I recommend that you continually complete as many of the following methods as you possibly can, depending on your strengths, preferences, and abilities. While you are working on these marketing methods, I urge you to keep your eyes and ears open to any possibility. When you are open and aware of all of your surroundings, you will find opportunities you never realized before!

To find what you seek in the road of life,
the best proverb of all is that which says:
"Leave no stone unturned."

~ Edward Bulwer Lytton

WORK ON YOUR MARKETING MATERIALS FIRST

Marketing materials are the items you will either be distributing to others, or pointing people towards. So, you will need to make sure they all look and sound professional and inviting, before you start directing potential clients and referral sources to them. It is important to appeal to your ideal client in order to have the most successful practice. The first, and most important, way to do this is with information placed on your marketing materials. You will need to have the following when starting your practice: business name, business phone number, voice mail greeting, professional e-mail address, website, brochure, professional-looking picture, business cards, and possibly fliers.

CHOOSE A BUSINESS NAME

The name you choose for your business is extremely important to the initial appeal of your practice. You may wish your practice name to be your full name and credentials, or you may choose another name for your practice. If you choose your own name you may want to include "& Associates" if you think you may hire others in the future. You may want your name included in the business name if there would be any type of recognition benefits for your practice. If you chose another name for your practice, you may want to choose one that will come up towards the top of alphabetical lists. It may also be a good idea to include your main service within the name of your business as it may come up quicker with some searches and clients might notice it sooner than they would with others. If you choose a name other than your own, it may benefit you if you sell your business because it may seem more attractive to the buyer, being named something else.

Either way, make sure it sounds inviting and professional. It is also a good idea for it to be a name that you could use ongoing without ever having to change it. Come up with some ideas and think about it for a while. Imagine you are a client seeing or hearing the name. I recommend running it by others (that you trust to be honest with you) to see how they think it sounds. A name can be quite psychological as it can sound very positive to potential clients, or it can be a slight "turn off" to the average client. For example, regular clients might find a name such as "Lighthouse Counseling" to be very professional, warm, inviting, and non-anxiety producing. In most cases, you will want the average client to feel "warm fuzzies" after seeing or hearing your practice name, like they may feel with "Lighthouse Counseling". Also it is a good idea to make sure your practice name is easily remembered so that people can find you again without much of a problem.

SET UP A BUSINESS PHONE NUMBER WITH A PROFESSIONAL-SOUNDING VOICE MAIL GREETING

You can do all the marketing in the world but if your voicemail greeting is not inviting and professional, I guarantee you will lose potential referrals. I cannot stress to you enough how important your voice mail greeting is to your business. This is usually the first impression potential clients and referral sources have of you and your practice, and the first time they will hear your voice.

Your greeting will need to tell callers they are contacting the right place and be inviting to them so they will want to leave a personal and confidential message. Making sure your greeting sounds professional, kind, and inviting is important. Sounding happy to receive their call and that you would be glad to speak with them is imperative. You can also ask them to say how they were referred, in their recording. Write down what you want to say as your script before you start recording. Then record and listen over and over until you feel you have the perfect greeting. Listen to it imagining you are a client or a referral source. Also have others listen to it and give honest feedback. Re-record yet again as many times as needed.

It is a good idea for this phone number to have the same area code as the clients you want to attract. When I worked as a referral counselor for managed care companies and Employee Assistance Programs, some clients did not want to call counselors that had a different area code than where they lived or where they thought the office was. It sounds strange, but you will lose some referrals by having an "out of area" area code.

Whenever you answer your phone live, make sure you sound professional, inviting, and kind. Again, I cannot stress this enough, because if they have a list of numbers to call, they call yours, and then you answer in an abrupt, non-professional way, most people will be turned off and may even hang up. Many people that are seeking help are feeling quite fragile and anxious, at least during their initial call. Some will be skittish, and any little thing that makes them feel uncomfortable may cause you to lose them as potential clients. This is particularly true for clients who have never tried counseling before. The whole process can be scary and intimidating.

As far as your phone goes, if you are going to be conducting telephone consultations, you will need to have a reliable land line, as it will be much clearer. The client will need to have one as well. I think all phones allow telephone number blockage by dialing "*67" first, so you may use your home phone. There are also ways to block call waiting from interrupting your session.

OBTAIN A PROFESSIONAL E-MAIL ADDRESS

It is possible to use your personal (existing) e-mail address for your business, as long as it sounds professional and inviting. I do not recommend using addresses that are meant to be cute or funny. I also do not recommend using a nickname that you have had. That would not be professional enough and could cost you referrals. My e-mail address just uses my professional name. It is easy to remember, which is also important to consider.

Remember to sign all of your e-mails with at least your full name, credentials, contact information, and web address. There will be many times when recipients of your e-mails will use the additional information for themselves, or forward it onto others.

CREATE A LOGO OR THEME AS WELL AS A STATEMENT

A practice logo, picture, theme, or statement can attract clients and make a business look more official. For example, for my practice we have a lighthouse picture theme and a statement that says "Helping you find your way". People seem to be attracted to those things. One woman just had to see us for her counseling because she loves lighthouses! I'll take that!

You can find logo pictures online. There are a few websites that allow people to download pictures for free. Of course, there are professionals that can help with this, for a fee. But, I urge you not to pay much for this.

As far as a statement or phrase goes, just think about what your whole practice symbolizes, or what you offer to people in general. Ask yourself: "What is the most important component?" Then come up with some phrases. Have others help you choose one or two from your list of possibilities.

OBTAIN A PROFESSIONAL-LOOKING PICTURE OF YOURSELF

You will need to have a nice picture of yourself, to use on your marketing materials. If you do not have any suitable pictures already, I would recommend using a digital camera (borrow one from a friend or family member if needed). Take as many shots as possible with different backgrounds, wearing some different shirts/suits, in different poses, and so forth. You might also look for reasonably-priced studios to help you. Perhaps there is a photographer in training who can work for a very low fee? It does not have to cost very much. Then ask people you trust which pictures they like the most (ask which ones look the most professional, inviting, and kind). Also put yourself in a client's shoes. Then look at your pictures and ask yourself "Is this someone I'd want to tell my life story to?" Also ask yourself "Does this person look competent, trustworthy, and kind?" Then choose the top one or two to have on your marketing materials. Make sure the picture is a close-up, is bright enough, and you are smiling in it. If you do not have a decent picture of yourself yet or are having difficulty with that aspect, I suggest you at least find a nice general picture to use such as a nature scene or comforting object, which you can probably find in a file on your computer. Nonetheless, you will need something for your website, online listings (which we will discuss later), and brochures. It is widely known that listings with pictures get more results. After all, "A picture is worth a thousand words".

DEVELOP A WEBSITE

Having a business website is necessary these days if you want to build your practice. First, see if someone you know can help you create or update your website. Otherwise ask around for some good and inexpensive services if you cannot do this yourself. I have seen some online listing sites that will help build a webpage. There are also some therapists who use a "page" on a paid listing site as their actual "website". They copy the specific web address link, and others can click on it to see their page. Although this is not the best option, it is much better than having no webpage at all. I have also seen situations where you can build a website for free. Again, do your research because there may be hidden costs and such. But, I am sure you will find something that fits with your ability as well as your budget. Being able to update your website relatively easily will be helpful, so keep that in mind as well.

Before developing or updating your website, it would be a good idea to check out as many other sites as possible. Therefore, review websites of other healthcare providers as well as other businesses. If you see something impressive or inviting, then write it down as something you generally want to include on your site. Also, if you see anything that that does not impress you or does not seem inviting, write those items down as well. You will want to use these notes to remind yourself of what you want on your site and what you do not.

Work with your programmer or web designer on entering your key words or "metatags". These are the search words that people are going to use to find you on the internet. So if you are doing this right, your list of key words will be extremely long. Make sure you include in your key words all of your roles such as "counselor". Also add what you do such as "psychotherapy". In addition, include what issues you work with such as "depression". You are also going to want to add every word that describes your office location(s) or the areas you serve, such as the state, town(s), neighborhoods, county, and region.

Ensuring your site is very professional, and has a nice picture of you, will yield more potential clients. Having bullet points and short, to-the-point, wording will help tremendously. Do not get too wordy as potential clients may have difficulty focusing on too much information and may feel overwhelmed. Put yourself in a potential client's shoes when looking at all your marketing materials. What would you like to see? What basic information would you like to know? What would be pleasing to your eyes if you were in crisis and looking for help? Understand that your target audience might not have any experience with the services you offer, so it would be a good idea to explain how your main services work. Also, include relaxing and soothing colors and pictures on your website and on other materials whenever possible.

You will have just a few seconds to draw in the viewer and communicate to them that they have found the right place. Therefore, you will want your business name at the top of the page, and under that have a very brief summary of who you are, what you do, and where you practice. Down further should be some sort of a "welcome" statement and then a few inviting sentences about your practice. Keep it concise and remove irrelevant words. Try to get as much information into a sentence as possible.

In the body of the website, I recommend that you have different sections arranged for easy reference. Such sections would include "Services Provided" as well as "Specialties". The "Services Provided" section could include bullet points with items such as "Individual, Couples & Family Counseling", "Hypnotherapy", "Telephone Counseling", "Home Visits", and so on. The "Specialties" section could include items such as "Depression/Anxiety", "Grief/Loss", "Relationships", "Coping with Physical Illness", and so on.

Including the number of years of clinical experience is also recommended. For social workers, we can begin the count at the second year internship, which is usually clinical. You may also want to add the total number of years of experience in your field as well. This number will be much larger than the number of clinical years, for most professionals.

Of course you are going to want all of your contact information easily accessible on your site, along with all of your office addresses. Having detailed directions and maps will be extremely helpful to your clients, as well as to you, as you can refer to them when you give out directions. You can discuss fees later when you are actually speaking with clients.

Let me say that your website does not have to be "high tech". In fact I think it is better if it is not. My website is quite simple and low tech. We have gotten many compliments on it and it draws in plenty of clients.

Your website does, however, need to be free of all errors. You will need to go through every sentence and statement, line by line, and make sure everything is error-free. Even if you have the site written for you, or there are pre-written sections, there still might be errors in grammar, spelling, and sentence structure. You are also going to want to make sure everything flows well for the potential reader. If you are not particularly strong in these areas, you are going to need a skilled person (or guide) to assist you with these tasks. There are excellent grammar guides at local libraries, or you can conduct a web search to find a grammar tutorial site. Just remember that errors and non-flowing sentences will turn off potential clients. By using correct grammar, readers will have more confidence in you as a professional.

Experiment with different font styles to see which one will be most inviting to your viewers. I am not sure why, but some font styles come across as more comforting and warm (perhaps non-aggressive), so it is something to consider. Keep this in mind for all of your written marketing materials, including all letters and e-mails.

Give your viewers a personal touch, letting "you" shine through. It is a good idea that your website has as much of "you" as possible, so that readers can see how it might be while in session with you. It would help to add something like an article or two that you have written. Be sure to also give some information on your site about what you are like in sessions so they can get more of a feel for it. This will help make it more original as well, which is tremendously important. We also want them to feel "warm fuzzies" from *you*.

I have not used Search Engine Optimization techniques (those services that are supposed to put your website on top of search engines), so I cannot speak on that. But if you come across what looks like a good situation, with a legit company and the rate looks good, you might want to give it a try as *one* of your marketing methods, along with manually placing your information on as many online listings as possible (focusing on your local area if that is what you are mostly targeting). There will be a significant amount of information about online listings later in this chapter.

Most professionals would agree that it is extremely important to have at least a basic website, even if you plan for your referrals to originate from elsewhere. I recently had a counselor, that I was doing consultation with, who thanked me for helping with her website. She said that even though all of her referrals were coming from a pediatrician's office, the mothers all wanted to see her counseling website before calling to schedule the first appointments for their children. So, this is something significant to consider, as it helps compel the potential client to take action and make the connection, so you can make the sale. In addition, a website may even be able to substitute for a brick-and-mortar establishment, depending on all that your business offers.

ORDER BUSINESS CARDS

My business cards are original, but professionally printed. I needed to do this because so many are required for the practice and we are constantly giving them out. I also think they should look professional, with quality materials, so I leave that to the printers. The large office supply stores offer business card services. Shop around for good deals in your area or online.

It is important to include your basic services on your card, so that the lay person understands basically what you do. Also include where you practice, at least the general area(s). My cards include my full name and credentials (letters behind my name), practice name, "Individual, Couple & Family

Counseling", "Offices in Naperville & Oswego, IL" my phone number, e-mail, website address, and "Helping you find your way". I would also recommend adding a small image if you can fit one on there. I would not waste space with things people can obtain later, such as fax numbers. If you are going to provide a way to write in the next appointment date and time, I would suggest having that printed on the back or having separate cards for that purpose only. You might as well add a brief statement about your cancellation policy while you are at it. With all of the information they contain, I can leave my business cards out in public places where this is allowed, and when someone sees the cards they know generally what I do and where. They can contact me or view the website and find more information if desired. This has worked out well.

I recommend purchasing a classy-looking card holder you can keep with you at all times. You never know when an opportunity will present itself and you will want to have your cards with you in a nice-looking card case.

CREATE BROCHURES AND FLIERS

See if it is possible to design and print your own brochures for your business. I make my own with my computer and copier. This way, I can update it easily with anything new. I use regular paper and black ink, all because it uses less resources and creates less waste that way. On my brochure, there is a lighthouse picture, our general services and specialties, techniques, all our contact information, towns our offices are in, payment options, and pictures of all the therapists. You might also cut and paste directions or a map to your office(s) if you have room. Being able to go in and change your brochures and fliers according to the expected audience or recipient, or when you add new credentials or services, will be helpful. Some will say to have at least two different brochures, one for potential clients and one for referral sources. You may consider this as it is not a bad idea. But, we have always had just one brochure and it has worked out just fine. If you have just one brochure, make sure it has the details needed by other professionals, but is understandable for the lay person as well. You may also consider additional brochures for larger separate services you may provide, or for areas where you are considered a specialist. Make sure they are professional-looking and inviting, with no errors. Like I say to the professionals I consult with, your brochure does not have to be awesome, but it does have to "be".

DISTRIBUTE YOUR MARKETING MATERIALS

It is imperative to make sure your practice information is available to anyone who might be in need of your services. Therefore, have your business cards and brochures in your waiting area. Also place your cards outside your office suite by affixing the card holder to your main door if possible. If you can also hang a brochure holder on or near your main office door, that would be beneficial as well. Potential clients and referral sources will probably see your office frequently and may want to take information at times when you are not there or your door is closed. I recommend placing your business cards everywhere it is allowed. When you are out and about, be aware of places where you can leave your cards out. I have my cards out in many places around my area, including the butcher, the health food store, the car wash, and many shops. If your cards look good, and you keep refilling them at the places you visit, you will most likely eventually get a few calls from potential clients. So, this method, since the only cost to you is the cards themselves, is well worth the effort! I have gotten calls and referrals from my cards that I have left at public places as well as outside my office door.

MARKET ON THE INTERNET WITH ONLINE LISTINGS

I cannot stress enough how online marketing can grow your practice. Having an online presence is extremely important, so I highly recommend using the internet as much as you possibly can. In addition to having a website with a long list of key words assigned, having several (as many as possible) professional-looking online listings will bring in a significant amount of referrals on an ongoing basis. A large number of potential clients are searching the internet for therapists and other service providers. What they are doing in many cases is using major search engines and typing in what they are looking for, such as "Counselor Naperville Illinois". Websites of professionals, as well as sites that list professionals, will then come up.

Suppose you are a woman with depression and you see an advertisement for depression therapy in your newspaper. If you are not ready to call then and there, that ad will go into the recycle bin. A month later you might be ready to call and will most likely search for a list of depression therapists in your area. The counselors who are on the lists you are viewing will be the ones you call. Therefore, seeing it from a potential client's perspective shows why being on lists (such as online listings) is so beneficial to businesses.

Some high quality websites actually offer free listings, some just require a link-exchange, and some others have a fee. Beware of expensive listing services: I would be careful about paying too much for any listing service where it is not known what you are going to receive, especially if you will be automatically billed in an ongoing manner. If there is one that you think will yield results, try to get a better rate by discussing with them before signing up. You can find out if it may yield results by doing searches for the main themes of the site, and perhaps the area it serves, to see if the site comes up at all. You can also contact a few business owners already listed to ask them briefly if they have been happy with their membership. You will want to contact someone who is not in competition with you though, in order to get a truthful answer. If you ask professionals who are listed in your area and provide the same services, they may want to discourage you from joining because you would be taking referrals that would have normally gone to them. They might not even realize that they are trying to discourage you, but it can happen.

If you are going to have to pay more than $25 total for a listing, spend time making sure it comes up in search engines, and somewhat high on the list, otherwise you might be wasting your money (if there would be no other benefits to you besides a listing). Some sites that charge approx $20 or $30 per month might result in a decent amount of referrals without doing much work, although sometimes you might feel like you are getting a lot of inquiries and no actual clients. You can negotiate the rate, ask for a discount, or see if they are having any specials or promotions. For example, if the listing fee is $60 per month, if they are not having any specials, talk with them and let them know that it would be difficult for you to pay that much per month. Ask if they can cut the fee in half. If they cannot, can they take $20 off per month? How about $10 off? If they cannot decrease the fee, what else can they do for you? What can they throw in to help sweeten the deal to get you to sign or continue with them? Can they designate you as a "Featured Professional" or "Therapist of the Month"? Some will be quite accommodating, and you will end up saving a bunch of money, or getting extras (or extra attention), for free. Always make sure a listing site is legitimate before you give any money or any credit card information.

Always make sure your listings are professional-looking and make you stand out from the crowd. Have others view your listings and give you honest feedback. Do this especially with your paid listing pages. A professional-looking picture of you usually will yield more potential referrals. At the very least, if you are not using a picture of yourself, add a nice picture such as a nature scene to listings that allow pictures. Just click "browse" on the listing screen which should take you to pictures already on your computer. Having your listings link to your website will be quite helpful in building your practice, so you will want to make sure to include your website any time possible. Do not get too wordy on listings as potential clients may have difficulty focusing on so much information and may feel overwhelmed. Again, keep your marketing materials concise and remove irrelevant words. Try to pack as much information into a sentence as possible. Put yourself in a potential client's shoes when creating your listings.

Make sure you list all the services that you can possibly offer (e.g., Individual, Couples & Family Counseling for Clients of All Ages; Hypnotherapy & Holistic Approaches; Seminars; In-Office, Online, Phone & On-Site Consultation). If you are a psychotherapist, be sure to include that you provide help for depression and anxiety. Potential clients do not always know that all psychotherapists work with depression and anxiety, so be sure to include a bit about that.

There are countless online listing sites that are absolutely free of charge! As mentioned earlier, some might just require an exchange link, where you also place their website on your site's information section (which can increase your online rankings). You never know when you can hit the jackpot as well, when you have a free listing that renders results. Ahhhh, what a great feeling! To find these online listings, simply go to all of the major search engines, and type in the search phrases that your potential clients may use. For a few examples, here are some words I have typed in <u>for my own marketing searches</u>:

- "Counselor in Naperville, IL"
- "Marital Therapist near Naperville, Illinois"

- "Addictions Counselor Naperville"
- "LCSW Western Suburbs Chicago"
- "Psychotherapist List"
- "Anger Management USA"
- "Depression Help"
- "Holistic Counselors USA"
- "Hypnotists Illinois"
- "Free Listings for Psychotherapists"
- "Free Therapist Listings USA"
- "Free Business Listings for Services"
- "Naperville Business Directory"

Brainstorm and come up with all of the words a potential client (or referral source) might use to search for you. Then, type each of them into all major search engines. Obviously there are endless possibilities to what a "potential" would type in to find you, so it could actually take quite a while to find most of the sites out there. When you find some free sites, add your information as you feel comfortable. If you are doing this right, you will find countless sites to list your practice. Do not be afraid to ask a site how to list your information if the instructions are not easily found. Keep the name of each site on hand, as well as your passwords. You will want to be able to go back and update your listings when needed, and you will then have a record of where you have added your practice information. Also save in your computer what you wrote about your practice so you can easily go back and cut and paste into the next listings where you are adding your information, especially if you were happy with the way it all sounded. However, try to tailor each entry to the particular listing where you are adding your information. So if it is a marital site, add what makes you a marital expert, and what services you have that relate to couples and families. Always go back and check your entries to make sure everything is correct and looks appealing.

A word of caution when placing your information online: try to make sure the site will not sell your information to mailing lists. You have the right to ask them not to do this. From my experience, it has been the larger, more well-known, sites that sell information. Another option, if you see an increase in junk mail after you have done some online marketing, is to ask them how they received your information. Then make sure that source does not continue to sell your information to mailing lists. By that time though, it may be a bit too late and you may have some additional junk mail for a few years until that previous mailing list is considered outdated by the mailing lists themselves. Until then, you may have to deal with it. So just do what you can to minimize the junk mail, otherwise you will find it is like a full-time job just keeping up with your mail!

Another potential problem with placing your information online is that very rarely you may receive an inappropriate or unwanted contact via phone or e-mail. But, I would say the majority of the people who contact us are legitimate potential clients.

You may also come across a site where readers can rate a listed service or product. Your business might actually already be listed on a site like this (sometimes information gets uploaded automatically). You can search your name and see what comes up. If you find your information on one of these sites, and you are okay with being on the site, then register and update your profile. If you really do not want to be on a site like this, then you can ask if they can remove your information.

I have done some link-exchanges where it was good and helpful information to have on my site as well. So, if you agree to place their website on yours, you get a free listing on their site. I would recommend this if you think it would be beneficial for you. You could have a section named "Other Helpful Sites" on your website, or a resources page where you can add your link exchanges. **I recommend that you do as many free listings as possible, a few link exchanges, and also a few reasonably-priced paid listings.**

As mentioned earlier, it is important to give readers a personal touch, letting "you" shine through in your listings. Also be sure to give statements about how you are in sessions so they can get more of a feel for how it might be working with you, again more "warm fuzzies".

After you have added your information to several online listing sites, wait several days and then type in the same search information. As the web crawls to your listings, you will begin seeing yourself come up on the searches! Then potential clients will be able to find you these ways as well. Also type in your name and then practice name, to see when they start coming up online! Note that some of your previous clients will search your name to find you again in the future, so you are going to want to be there so they can easily find you again.

START INTERNET BLOGS ABOUT YOUR PRACTICE

There are many positive things being said about online blogs for marketing a business. So whenever you have a chance to set up and keep a blog, take it. I have set up a few blogs for my practice, all for free. I think they generate a great deal of interest in the practice, which is current and updated. With blogs, it is recommended that you write at least two posts per month (short posts are fine). You can input announcements into your blogs which will be useful. I have heard that blogs can increase one's search engine rankings, meaning you will come up faster when someone searches for a service you provide in your area. So, search engines seem to like blogs, probably because the information is constantly being updated. It is also possible to have systems that track certain things such as what posts your visitors read, which can be useful.

CONTRACT WITH REPUTABLE EMPLOYEE ASSISTANCE PROGRAM (EAP) COMPANIES

If you are a mental health professional, consider EAPs for practice-building. (If you are not a mental health professional, see the end of this section for other opportunities EAPs may provide for you). EAPs contract with businesses to provide counseling for their employees and family members. The counseling is already pre-paid by the employer. We are EAP affiliates for many EAPs who need to provide counselors for businesses/employees in our area. We tend to see an increase in EAP referrals during economic downturns, as people are feeling more and more stressed in their jobs, numerous employees are being laid off, and many do not have a lot of extra money for therapy. On a related note, we also see an increase in requests for career-oriented counseling, which has been an interesting trend and a need we are filling.

As EAP affiliates, our main roles are providing assessments, short-term counseling, and referrals to employees and their family members. If you are interested in this type of work, you can find EAP companies by doing online searches and asking around. It is a good idea to run the company names by others in order to get more information on their reputations. There are a few that I have learned to stay away from, but for the most part they are good. When contacting these companies, ask if they are in need of affiliate counselors in your area. Some of these applications are lengthy, so make sure there is a need and also that you would qualify to be in their network, before completing the credentialing materials. If there is no current need in your area, ask if they will keep your basic information on file in case they are in need in the future, as you may get a referral (or even a contract) this way. Also, before contacting them, make sure you have an updated resume ready to send, as most EAPs will require a resume. Make sure to highlight all of your most important credentials, education, and specialties, including how long you have been practicing. I recommend keeping your resume to two pages or less.

If you are in a rural area, do not assume there are no EAP opportunities for you. For example, labor unions and manufacturing companies, as well as county and state government organizations, frequently utilize EAP-type services for their members or employees. In addition, within the transportation industry (e.g., trucking and railroads), certain types of EAP services are often required for employees.

With most EAPs, you will have to be willing to do assessments, referrals, short-term counseling, and clinical paperwork. Many also require a certain type of experience, and most require an independent license. But, there are a few that only require a masters degree in the field of mental health (supervised by a fully licensed clinician) as well as a desire to follow their procedures. With those you can gain the EAP experience if you do not have any yet.

One aspect that many clinicians do not realize is that with many EAPs you are allowed to self-refer cases. This means that after the assessment (or short-term counseling) is done you may refer to yourself for the ongoing counseling treatment (if it is a good match and is needed). Therefore, this is a huge referral source that many therapists do not think of. Many times I hear from counselors "I don't want to take that rate or do the paperwork", but what they are not thinking of is how they can self-refer those clients into their practice resulting in a growing caseload of long-term insurance and self-pay (sometimes full-fee) clients. So I look at this as another form of marketing, but where you actually get paid for building your practice! How can a new therapist ask for anything more? We have also seen a number of these EAP clients refer friends and family to our practice because they received good quality care from us.

Another aspect that most clinicians do not realize is that it is possible to negotiate EAP rates. Initially, before the contract is signed, and then later after you have done some good work for them (usually at least a year), you can request higher rates. You may or may not get the answer you would like to hear, but it is worth asking. I suggest requesting a little higher rate than what you would actually accept. This is because what they usually do (if they will be raising it at all) is meet you in the middle, somewhere between the current rate and the rate you requested. Always discuss these issues with respect, also highlighting your special abilities that make you stand out from the crowd. Some of these may include certain specialties such as working with children, providing marital counseling, having addictions expertise, being bilingual, having an office in a remote area for underserved clients, having current evening and weekend times, and so forth. Put yourself in their shoes to see what they may like to hear.

One other positive trait of EAPs is that as long as the authorization is in place in your name, you will get paid for your service and in the expected amount, which is not always the case with insurance and client payments. Some EAPs also reimburse for missed appointments. In addition, with EAPs you will not have to mess around with collecting client copays. This can be quite refreshing!

It is important to keep a positive relationship with each company and the referring case managers. Being responsive and cooperative will get you far in the world of EAP (and managed care for that matter). You can also send over brief letters periodically, reminding referral or intake counselors that you have current openings. Include a few business cards for them to distribute and keep by their desk for easy referrals. You may even want to attach some business cards to magnets so they can keep them in their cubicle for quick and easy referrals.

EAPs can also provide avenues to providing other services such as Critical Incident Stress Debriefings (CISDs), onsite counseling (at job sites), management consultation, SAP evaluations (Substance Abuse Professionals for DOT referrals), educational seminars (e.g., stress management), and running health fair booths. These tasks can be quite interesting and can nicely break up a typical week (with good pay I might add!). Again, negotiate your fee, as well as reimbursable items when you can.

Other bits of information and advice: If there is an EAP that does not usually allow self-referrals, still consider them. Not only will it increase your chances of being called for work, but you will still be able to get your name out to others in many ways, and also get paid for services. An additional aspect to keep in mind here is that if you do a considerable about of EAP work, then you would be considered a referral source by other professionals, which is a perfect ice-breaker when networking. Another bit of information is that there are a few EAPs that also do managed mental healthcare ("managed care") for health insurance companies, in addition to the EAP piece.

If you are not a mental health professional, there are still some opportunities with certain EAPs. If you are any type of service provider, do some research to see if you can have a connection with EAPs. I know that they frequently have referral services, usually called "Work Life Services" where employees can be linked to all types of professionals. Service providers under "Work Life Services" programs or networks typically include providers not covered by health insurance, such as legal, financial, child and elder care, cleaning, and more. If you are any type of professional coach (such as an executive coach), I have seen a few EAPs contract with, and sometimes even cover, these services as well

CONTRACT WITH REPUTABLE INSURANCE AND MANAGED CARE COMPANIES

If you have a license or certification that is reimbursable by health insurance, then I would recommend obtaining a few insurance or managed care contracts, at least in the very beginning of your practice. Research and ask around to see what plans seem to be high quality and have considerable amounts of members in your area. Start with the major insurers (or managed care companies) first and then go from there. When you obtain the contact information for the companies (from other therapists, online, or from client benefit information), ask the provider relations department if they are in need of providers in your area. If so, then ask how you can become contracted to be in-network. Like with EAPs, some of these applications are lengthy so make sure you would qualify for their network, and there is a need in your area, before completing the credentialing materials. If there is not a current need in your area, ask if they will keep your basic information on file in case there is a need in your area in the future, as you may get a referral, or even a contract, this way.

With many insurance plans, if you are in-network you may get referrals straight from the insurance or managed care company itself. Also, many of them have their provider networks online and in books for potential clients to peruse. With all the plans you are on, make sure that you are listed appropriately and in all areas that you should be listed. For example, I remember looking up my name on some provider lists and finding that one had me listed as a male, one had the spelling of my last name incorrect, and many did not have my secondary office address listed.   These issues cost me several referrals, I am sure. So, check into all the lists you should be on and speak with the provider relations representative as soon as possible if anything needs to be corrected. The same goes here, as in EAPs, where you will want to make sure your name and contact information is always in front of the referring case managers! In addition, if you get a referral from somewhere else and during the initial intake conversation it is found that you are in-network for the client's insurance, it is almost like a shoe-in from there. It is quite a nice ice-breaker!

Managed care/insurance rates are also negotiable in many cases, especially if you provide services to an underserved area, have the specialties the provider relations department needs to fill, have considerable experience, or the rate is low to begin with. So, do not just sign any contract that is in front of you, especially if you are not satisfied with it. Negotiate, negotiate, negotiate!

If you decide to work with any insurance or managed care companies, make sure it is placed on your marketing materials. On my brochures, website, and many listings I have "Insurance, EAP, Cash/Checks, & Credit/Debit Cards Accepted". It may also help to list the specific plans you are in-network with, whenever possible.

JOIN ASSOCIATIONS OF INTEREST

I have found some health-related associations which are free or low cost to join. I recently found an association for hypnotists and was able to join for free. They also gave me an online listing, as well as a certificate to hang in my office. All for free! All I had to do was a link-exchange. Who could ask for anything more? So, search for associations that interest you, which provide free or low cost membership. Even if it is just something you place on your marketing materials and listings, it will make you look official, will add to your credentials, and will give a message for "potentials" to see as to your interests and specialties. Some of the larger professional associations can be a bit pricey, but if you see that you will receive many benefits from joining, then I would recommend it. Some provide free CEUs (Continuing Education Units), insurance at a discount, or other useful perks. So some memberships are well worth the cost. Some others you may want to join just for the sake of getting information and donating to a cause (e.g., cancer or celiac disease). Do not forget to place those memberships on your listings and other marketing materials as well. They can show a particular interest, knowledge, or approach that at potential client might appreciate.

NETWORK WITH OTHER PROFESSIONALS

Most private practice professionals desire to branch out and meet others, especially if they are somewhat new in practice. That said, I do want to make sure you do not let one "turn down" or failed reach out get the best of you. Get right up and work on the next marketing task!

Keep your options open. Consider networking with any type of professional, either by finding existing networking groups, or by reaching out to other professionals that you have met before or would like to meet. If you have a mutual client already, then you have an "easy in". Take any opportunity as it will be helpful in developing any type of networking relationship. Also look for something you might have in common as an "easy in" such as office space, certification, schooling, age, past employment, and so forth. Look at what they offer and if you offer something a bit different, then you may not be in direct competition, and can refer to each other! In addition, if you offer some of the same services, but that counselor has to refer out sometimes for any reason, she can refer to you. You can also search for local meetings and seminars in order to meet others. Also, try to arrange meetings with other helping professionals such as school social workers if you work with children and adolescents. Try to put yourself in their shoes. What do they need as far as referral resources? How can I connect with them and make sure they know I can fill those needs in the area? How can I make their job easier and make them look good? That is what you will want to do in order to get their referrals. For example, a physician that works with adults might be very interested in referring to a hypnotist that offers services such as smoking cessation. Keep your mind open to all the possibilities!

Professionals are going to look for specific items in your announcements and other marketing materials. They will look for specialties that are hard to find. Then they will attach, in their mind, your name to those specialties and populations served, in order to help themselves with their own practices (for giving quality referrals and such). So think about what you would want them to connect with you such as: "Your Name-- children, disabled, autism, expressive therapy, traditional therapy, motherhood, postpartum, caregivers". Be sure to have enough information, but still keep it concise.

I would not recommend sending fliers or letters to random professionals or organizations as it probably will not yield enough results, especially for how time-consuming and costly it can be. If you do go this route though, it *does* have to be more than just sending one brochure, in order to get results. I have read several times that this method will not yield referrals *unless* the people you are sending them to are at least somewhat familiar with you. I think that professionals are reluctant to refer to others that they do not know. We have tried this many times and, honestly, I do not think it really ended up in any real referrals (except maybe one or two). Other professionals that need to refer to you will find you if you are on the client's insurance network or have a specialty or location that is needed. As long as you have worked enough on the recommended marketing methods in this book, they will be able to find you!

If you know of, or are networking with, a professional such as a dietician, psychiatrist, physician, executive coach, chiropractor, attorney, or health food store owner, ask if they want to exchange cards and brochures. Therefore, it would be the understanding that you would refer to each other. Do this only with others that you feel comfortable referring to, and who you feel would refer to you as well. You might also consider exchanging endorsements with another professional.

As mentioned earlier, keep in mind that if you do a considerable amount of EAP work, then you would be considered a referral source by other professionals, which is a perfect ice-breaker when networking.

Suppose another professional contacts you and wants to give information or ask questions in order to help *herself*. Try not to get upset by these types of situations, because they can be a great opportunity for *you*! You can use it as a perfect segway into telling *her* about *your* practice and anything you might be able to offer her or others she knows. Discovering how she found you will be valuable knowledge gained as well. This could also be the start of a new friendship. You never know!

There are many business networking opportunities online. They usually have a theme such as "holistic health practitioners", "social workers", or "mental health". There are some general business networking sites as well. Some are local, and some are more national or international. Many of these types of sites allow free listings, networking with others, e-mail distribution, business announcements, and ad postings. They also usually have certain groups you can join within the site, such as "private practice marketing", which can help you get exposure, and allow you to learn new ideas from others as well.

There are some other groups that meet at local places. You can usually find this type of situation by searching for your local "Meetup" groups.

I have not tried "cold-calling" anyone on the phone, except EAP and managed care companies to see if they were in need of providers, and that worked well (even with my introverted personality type!). I do not recommend cold-calling, other than that, unless perhaps your plan is to call other professionals and you are an extravert personality type.

Please note that it might take some time to get a referral from a given source. It may take one to two years for an opportunity to present itself to a professional you are networking with. So, just be patient and the fruits of most your networking labors will eventually pay off.

Networking is building a people resource bank that pays interest and dividends that compound annually for as long as you're alive.

~ Jeffrey Gitomer

FIND OUT WHAT OTHERS ARE DOING

Great inspiration can be gained by viewing the marketing materials of other professionals, including their websites, yellow pages ads, and any other materials you can get your hands on (exchange brochures!). Also ask them if they have any advice for you, and ask other more specific questions as well. See what information you can get. If they are attracting referrals, maybe they will tell you how they are getting some of them? This may cost you a lunch or a coffee somewhere, but the information is like gold! A word of caution: Do not copy anyone. There are two major reasons why you should not copy anything. One is that they will likely find out that you took something from their marketing materials. Whether it is the look and background of a website, or certain wording in a yellow pages ad, they will likely find out. This can cause conflict, especially with those that are in your immediate area. For example, they may be hesitant to give referrals to you, because they see that you copied something from their website. The other major reason not to copy others is that you want to stand out from the crowd, not blend in to the crowd!

"WORD OF MOUTH" WORKS!

If you provide helpful quality services, then your clients will usually want to tell others about it. If they ever bring up the subject of referring people to you, thank them immediately and then give them some of your cards to distribute. Let them know that you love getting new clients and how well things are going in your practice. People are attracted to passion and positivity.

There are certain populations where "word of mouth" travels particularly well. Those populations include: employees, couples, parents of child/adolescent cases, and gay populations.

INFORM EVERYONE YOU KNOW

Inform everyone you know (I mean everyone) about your services, that you have room for a few new clients, and that you like getting referrals. Make statements like "I just love getting new clients" or "We love referrals" and "We're doing really well with such and such". Keep it short, sweet, very positive, and exciting. In the past, at a dentist's office I saw a sticker that said

"We Love Referrals" and I thought it was a really nice way for them to get their message across. A word of caution here: Save any desperate feelings or venting for people that you can trust, who can also give you support in return. Clients, potential clients, and referral sources do not fall into this category! But, in general I have found people to be genuinely interested, fascinated at times actually, during conversations about what I do. Keep your cards on hand in case there is an appropriate situation to give them out. Remember that even if you are not actually going to be seeing someone (due to "closeness", specialty, or location) you can still give out another professional's information and have the client give your name to them as "how they were referred". That other professional or organization will remember this, which may result in a referral back to you in the future.

Sending professional letters via mail or e-mail to people who know you may also help. It is important to send them to people that already know you at least somewhat, because if you send them to people who do not know you at all, and there is no follow-up in person or via phone, they will be very unlikely to refer to you, I have found. So make sure that when you are sending letters, the recipients know you already or will know you soon. Send information again to the same people informing them of anything new with your practice.

USE SOCIAL NETWORKING SITES

There are many social networking sites that have come about that provide opportunities to market a business. One large social networking site lets you start a page for your business, run promotions, post polls, and more. Some let you broadcast your activities and remind friends about your business. So, do some research to see which social networking sites you might want to use. I know that some of you do not want to mix business with your social life and that is completely understandable. However, if you do not mind doing this (having friends and family as a referral source) at least initially, and you think you could be successful at it, by all means do it. This is definitely a way to get more business, and it does not usually cost any money!

CONNECT WITH LOCAL SCHOOL SOCIAL WORKERS AND UNIVERSITY COUNSELING CENTERS

If you work with children, adolescents, or young adults, connecting with school-related professionals can be a fruitful activity. They are constantly referring to counselors in the community for treatment. I have found school employee contact information to be easily obtainable online. You will need to have excellent marketing materials, which should include your picture. I also strongly recommend that you at least speak with each of your contacts on the phone so they can get to know you and your services. Also request that they place your information on any resource lists they may have. Meeting face-to-face, in addition to direct mailings and phone conversations, will increase your chances of getting referrals. Again, I have found that referral sources are much more likely to refer to professionals with whom they have established a relationship. So, just sending one e-mail or a brochure is not likely going to get you any results.

CONTACT HOSPITALS AND OTHER FACILITIES

Contact the assessment professionals, case managers, counselors and discharge professionals at healthcare facilities to see how you can be included on their resource and referral lists. They are constantly referring or linking patients up with outpatient professionals. You can make their job much easier by informing them of all your services and locations, and being responsive to the needs of their referrals! If you provide any sliding scale fee reductions, also inform them of that, as well as all insurance/managed care networks you are on. Thank them for giving out your name, when appropriate, and if you have not heard from them in a while, remind them again of your services (make sure they always at least have your business cards and website address).

CONSIDER YOUR LOCAL CHAMBER OF COMMERCE

Chamber of Commerce groups have always intrigued me. I have not joined any yet, so I cannot comment on the results you may expect from joining one. But, you may want to look into that for yourself if you think you would like the social and networking aspect of your local Chamber. I think you would need to have the willingness to participate in the social and networking events in order to make your membership worthwhile. I do know the ones around my offices seem a bit pricey, but if they could decrease their fees, and you would enjoy the social aspects, then it would probably be worth it. You also can ask other members if they have been happy with what they have gotten from their membership. Chamber memberships do make businesses look official and "locally involved" which is always positive, I do have to say. They also seem to have an internet presence, which is another positive aspect.

WRITE ARTICLES OR GIVE PROFESSIONAL QUOTES

There are many ways one can submit articles to online sites, newspapers, magazines, and such. Make sure the articles are brief, professional, and inviting. It also is usually a good idea for them to cover topics that relate to common subjects that the general public would appreciate. It is imperative that all of your contact information and credentials appear in the article, and that it is clear that anyone could contact you for services. See how many sites and papers you can submit to, by simply asking! Many allow free submissions, and a few papers do pay if you become a columnist. You can also contact newspapers, magazines, and websites to see if anyone would like to interview you for any upcoming articles. I have been contacted countless times by columnists for professional quotes for their articles. This happens because they know where to find me, can see my credentials easily, know that I like doing interviews, and know I am available. After the articles are printed, I always thank the columnists and compliment them on their writing.

With all of your professional quotes, make sure you include your full name, credentials, general titles (e.g., psychotherapist & hypnotist), practice name, office locations (at least general areas), phone number, e-mail, and website. News organizations are dealing with a lot of information and you will need to spoon-feed them in order to ensure it goes to print correctly. Although it is possible to go back and instruct them to print corrections later, it is much more desirable to have your full correct information included in the article itself. I also recommend having them e-mail or send over their questions beforehand, thereby giving you time to be prepared for the interview.

You should not pay the news organizations to be able to do this; you will be spending time on these articles and giving your expertise, so you should not be paying to have them printed, in my opinion.

If there happen to be some interesting articles you were involved with, that went to print and got positive feedback, then have them professionally framed for your office. You can also make copies of them and place them in literature holders for your waiting room. You will look incredibly official displaying or distributing any of your quality publications! It is also recommended that you place your articles, or links to your articles, on your you will attract clients who are in need of services related to those topics. They can also grasp more of a feel for how services would be with you after reading them, which may result in an appointment.

PLACE BUSINESS ANNOUNCEMENTS IN NEWSPAPERS

Most people do not know that placing business announcements in local papers is completely free! Hard to believe, isn't it? So whenever you have something new happen, whether it is opening an office, getting a new certification, offering additional services, or participating in an upcoming event, submit it to all of your local papers' business announcement sections.

Business announcements work especially well in smaller cities and towns where they may be looking for news. It might also work with smaller papers within big cities (such as neighborhood newspapers). So check into all the possibilities with your local papers and online news sources. You can find many local news sources by searching online as well as at your local library. Also look into papers that serve communities within 30 minutes of your office locations. This will work particularly well if you offer "hard to find" techniques or services that people cannot find in their own area. Adding "telephone sessions" to your list of services will help for those who live far. In addition, you could offer longer sessions to farther-away clients.

You will want to keep your announcements short and concise, with a catchy phrase for the headline. For example, I just submitted one to my local papers announcing "Local Counselor Becomes Certified Hypnotherapist". In the body of the announcement, briefly explain the important details, then give all of your contact information and credentials at the bottom. I think you can also include a picture with most business announcements, which would attract more readers.

I have found it easiest to submit these business announcements via e-mail; the addresses can be found in the papers or on their websites. Request that your announcement be placed in the business section for their next printing. They may not respond directly to you, but watch the papers, because you will likely see your announcements printed. Keep each paper's contact information so you can easily submit your next batch of announcements when something new comes up again.

Announcements can attract clients and referral sources, increase credibility, as well as help maintain essential contact with media. Having a loyal base of people familiar with your business helps ensure a healthier bottom line.

SUBMIT YOUR GROUPS, CLASSES, AND OTHER SERVICES TO NEWSPAPERS

If you can offer certain ongoing services such as anger management classes or groups, then send this information to your local newspapers that have "social services" or "support" pages. When you are reading your local papers, be aware of any lists where your services may relate. Contact the newspaper to find out how to add your services to a specific list. From my experience, these listings are free and ongoing, even if you are for-profit. If you do not obtain enough clients for an actual class or group, you can always offer one-on-one service to any callers. I have also seen "Human Services" pages in our local newspapers and have submitted some practice information to those pages. My practice information has been there for years now.

OFFER SEMINARS OR CLASSES

If you happen to be a dynamic speaker who feels comfortable in front of a crowd, you can use this skill to grow your business by offering classes or seminars. However, this is not for everyone. If you dread public speaking, and are uncomfortable in front of a group, this will show, and make it difficult to win new clients this way. Focus on what you like to do, as there are plenty of other activities that will get the clients in. But, if you do like public speaking and are an energetic and engaging speaker, take advantage of that! Also perhaps there are one or two topics on which you feel comfortable speaking. If you go around and do a few of these, you will likely see results rather quickly. Make sure at the end of your seminars you have your cards available and you make it known how to reach you. Also note that you are in private practice in the area and are taking new clients.

These presentations may have to be provided for free, at least at first. Look at it as free marketing. Make it easy for yourself and target already formed groups in your area that would make ideal clients for you. For example, locate and contact local divorce support groups if you want to grow your "divorce recovery" practice. Contact children's grief support groups if you want to work with childhood grief and loss. Contact parenting support groups if you want more child and family referrals.

It is possible to set up a seminar and charge a small fee. But doing it this way will take much planning and marketing, and it may not be completely worthwhile for you when it is all said and done. If you are really interested in doing this, go ahead and give it a try, as it might work, especially if your office is located in a large city. I just have not completed a task like this from beginning to end so I cannot speak on its entirety.

There are also ways to sign up to be a Continuing Education seminar provider, so if you think professionals would refer to you due to having unique specialties, do some research on how to become a CEU provider in your area (or join a group that offers them). This can be an excellent way for referral sources to get to know you. You can also receive payment for conducting CEU seminars, which is a bonus. Offering tele-classes (classes held via telephone) may also be an option.

I have also heard that teaching a class at a college or university can give exposure as well as extra income. Some teaching positions may also provide employee benefits as well.

Of course, there are opportunities within EAPs providing seminars to businesses in your local area. Some typical topics include: stress management, EAP benefit orientation, diversity in the workplace, balancing work and family, and coping with change. EAPs typically pay well for seminars, and they are usually pre-written which makes it much easier. You might not be able to distribute your own business cards at these seminars due to needing to look like a representative from the EAP, but you might receive EAP referrals after these, and you also may be able to give your cards to those that request them.

People who want to improve on their public speaking can join groups like Toastmasters or Optimist Club. There are usually local chapters everywhere. Involvement in these types of organizations can also improve writing and other communication skills, which are added benefits.

HAVE MORE THAN ONE OFFICE LOCATION

At least initially, it is quite helpful to have two office locations. You will likely build up faster by giving clients more choice and drawing clients from two different areas. It might also be possible to negotiate a higher rate with

EAPs and managed care companies because they will likely need you more if you have two locations. Therefore it can be advantageous for leverage. It can also be helpful for attracting more of the type of referrals you desire (or to fill a certain time of day over another). I would suggest that you choose locations that either have high populations, or areas that are lacking in the services or specialties/techniques you provide, and you can fill that need.

CHECK INTO EVERYTHING YOUR OFFICE BUILDING CAN POSSIBLY DO FOR YOU

It may surprise you to discover all the ways the staff at your office building can help. Look into signage as well as presence on the building's website if possible. In our Naperville office, we have made sure we are listed on both of the directories in the building along with our credentials. In our Oswego office, we are listed on the directory by the front door and I had them add "Counseling & Therapy" under our practice name. At the time of this writing, we are also listed as one of the businesses on the building's website, along with a link to our website! There are also parties and networking opportunities held there as well. If you have any of these opportunities within your office building, I highly suggest you take advantage of them. If you cannot make it to a party or meeting, request that they at least display your brochures and cards at the event. After all, it benefits them if you are doing well.

HANG OUT IN YOUR OFFICE DURING "DOWN" TIMES

I know this does not sound like much fun, but when you are not seeing clients, consider staying in your office with the doors open and the lights on. Do some reading or paperwork in there and listen for anyone who might be walking around or coming to the door to check out your services. This works particularly well in buildings where there are many therapists. Some people I have met this way have actually told me they came to the building to "therapist shop"! This may also work in buildings where there are usually people milling around. Eventually, you will have someone wanting to talk with you, but you will have to give it a bit of time. Remember, anyone can be a referral source as well, so be open to all possibilities! As always, have your brochures and cards in the waiting room ready to be given to the potential clients.

DOES YOUR CHURCH RUN ADVERTISEMENTS?

My church allows ads to be placed in their bulletin for just $1.00 per month. So I just submit my business card and pay for how many times I would like them to run it (usually for several months). As mentioned earlier, my business cards already have my credentials, contact information, website, and my general services on them. Therefore, this can be an extremely easy and inexpensive way to market yourself if you are affiliated with any churches.

PROVIDE SERVICES THAT ARE DIFFICULT TO FIND

Whether it is location, specialty, a certain technique, or a population served, if you are the only one doing it, you will get the referrals. I always recommend that a professional who wants to build her practice also continue learning new techniques and specialties according to her interests. For example, it might not be quite enough that someone is a Licensed Clinical Social Worker and does Cognitive Behavioral Therapy (CBT). If she also offers additional techniques or specialties such as hypnosis, that gives yet another pool of potential clients interested in seeing her. So, if a client is at all interested in discussing hypnosis as part of his treatment, he will likely choose the therapist that is also a certified hypnotist or similar.   Specializing in underserved populations will also be smart, such as offering services to lesbian and gay populations.   If   you   include   statements   such   as   "LGBT   Affirming Psychotherapy", "LGBT Friendly", or "LGBT Populations" on your marketing materials, these people will find you, and choose you over others. Also many clients need evening or weekend time slots and not every counselor provides that or has those times open. You will stand out in a crowd if you provide that without a wait.   The same might also go for credit card acceptance, office location, offering home visits, phone sessions, and more. Along these lines, be sure to put these items on all of your marketing materials so that potential clients can see them quickly and will call you and not the next person they see who clearly offers what they are looking for.

ALWAYS ASK "HOW DID YOU GET MY NAME?"

You are going to want to ask every potential client how they heard about you, and their responses should be considered like gold. You are going to need to know anyway, for clinical and payment purposes. But, knowing how they were referred is necessary for your future marketing and where you are going to want to focus even more energy. You are going to want to find out as much as you possibly can about how they found you. If they say "online", ask where, specifically. Also ask what they typed in for their search as that will give you even more information.   If someone referred the client, try to obtain consent from the client to formally thank the referral source. If you are getting inquiries referred by another therapist, then you might want to say something very general to him such as "I think you might be giving out my name and number and I just wanted to say thank you".

ALWAYS SAY "TELL THEM I SENT YOU"

"Tell them I sent you" is something you are going to want to always say if you are giving out someone else's practice or business information. Not only will the client likely get a response more quickly, but the receiver of the new client will not forget that you were the one who made it happen. They will probably return the favor sometime in the future with a referral or some type of assistance for you. Little things like this will definitely start adding up, making a substantial difference.

SEND GREETING CARDS

Send holiday cards to all of your referral sources that you would like to continue working with. Give them the message that you have enjoyed working with them and appreciated everything during the past year. Also say that you are looking forward to continuing that "relationship" into the next year as well. Most organizations have bulletin boards where they place their greeting cards, for all the referral counselors to see.

Also consider writing "thank you" notes to other professionals that have helped you or given you referrals. Send notes to columnists that have included your quotes in their articles. Compliment them on their writing and let them know you are available for more interviews in the future. You also may want to send brief "thank you" letters to specific case managers and referral counselors who have given you referrals. You usually will receive their names upon each referral, or on the client paperwork they send. Thank them for the referral and inform them that you have more openings. Enclose a few business cards.

ACCEPT MAJOR CREDIT CARDS

Seeing "credit cards accepted" on your marketing materials will look inviting, especially to self-pay clients or those with high copays or deductibles. Accepting credit cards has worked well for us in general, as we require at least $40 for the charge, so they cannot charge any less than that. If their copay is low they might have to pay their copays in bulk if they want to use their credit card. I do not recommend signing up to take credit cards if you do not have enough clients to make it worth it. Every plan is different, but from what I have seen, they have monthly fees in addition to the other fees such as a percentage of what was charged. So if you do not have many clients yet or no one has asked much about whether you take credit cards, then postpone this. If, however, you feel it is the right time to look into it, then do your homework and speak to a few different services to see what would be the best fit for you and at the lowest cost. If you do decide to accept credit cards, then place their logo signs on all of your marketing materials as well as on your office or suite door. Clients will be attracted to this.

PLACE ALL OF YOUR PAYMENT OPTIONS ON YOUR MARKETING MATERIALS

On your marketing pages, offer all payment options you would accept, such as insurance, EAP, credit and debit cards, cash, checks, bulk payments, and monthly payments. If you accept sliding scale fees, then make sure you state: "sliding scale fees are available if necessary". Discuss actual fees when you have the client on the phone.

At times, we actually get people calling asking if we take cash. They are not sure if we work exclusively with insurance companies or have some other type of set-up. So make sure they know that, yes, you definitely take cash!

PLACE A SMALL YELLOW PAGES AD OR BASIC LISTING

Yes, a few people are still looking at the yellow pages, whether they do not have access to the internet, their computer is down, they would rather use a book, or they just received the book and want to look at what they may need, it still happens. It is not an overwhelming amount anymore, but there still seems to be people out there looking through phone books. Therefore, for new or previous clients to find you, it might be helpful to have a small presence in the yellow pages.

I highly recommend first asking other business owners in your area if there are any reputable books in which it might be useful for you to place an ad. If you find that there is a reputable book and would like to place an ad, have them place it on the right side of the page if at all possible. It has been shown that people tend to look on the right side page first when they open a book. Make your services catch their eyes right away. For example, I might put "Licensed Professional Counseling & Hypnosis" in bold at the top of my ad, so that it explains what we offer and it catches their eye right away for people who are looking for that. I need to do this because the name of my practice is mainly my name and credentials, it does not have "counseling" or anything indicating what we do. It is also not a big enough name to be recognized by the lay person (not enough "name recognition"). Then, include your top specialties in your ad if possible (the specialties you want to attract the most). You will want people who are searching for something specific to see that you can help with their specific problems (such as "grief/loss"). Do not include more than twelve specialties. Including your website address in your ad is important, and if they will also be placing your listing or ad online, that would be another huge bonus. Also make sure your ad will look eye-catching to the type of clientele you would like to attract. Be sure to ask for help and feedback on your ad before you send it for print. Also have the book's marketing services help with your ad in any way possible.

I do not recommend buying a large ad space because I think it is too expensive for what you might receive from it. I am thinking about very small boxes or basic listings. I also do not recommend paying extra for color in your ad. I do, however, suggest that they throw in some way to make it stand out from others (for example, adding a different-shaped border, a darker outline around the ad, or some color).

Yellow pages ads can still be helpful in obtaining some new clients, but also for some others out there who already know you and just need to find your number. But, if you have been working diligently on most of the marketing methods in this book, which should be first, they will eventually find your contact information. It just might make it easier for them to have it from the phone book, thus resulting in you getting the calls, rather than someone else. Having a presence in the phone book will also make you look more official as an established business, to new and existing clients, which is always beneficial.

There is typically more than one book in a given area. Use this information as negotiation leverage. Play "hard to get" and also do not fall into any of their sales games. Feel free to say "no" to any salesperson about anything, and really think things through before signing anything. If they have come down to what seems to be their rock bottom on price, and they are adding some ways to make your ad stand out, ask what else they can do to sweeten the deal for you. Some ideas might be: adding you to additional categories (such as "addictions services" and "psychotherapists", when you are already going to be listed under "counselors"), upgrading the size of one or more of the ads, or adding an online listing.

TAKE SOME LOW-FEE CASES AT FIRST

Consider taking some low fee, sliding scale, cases. I suggest doing this especially if you are just starting out in your practice or you need to build up fast. Look at it like getting paid to market your services, because if the clients you are servicing are happy with what you provide, they will tell others about you.

Some therapists use a sliding scale rule of charging $10 per every $10k in the annual household income. So, if the income is $60k, the cost of a session would be $60. Of course there will have to be a minimum you would take because it obviously cannot be zero or $10 (unless you wanted to do that for a case for some reason). But at least that gives some type of method or rule of thumb instead of making guesses on what should be charged. (Also see Chapter Four under "Some Additional Tips on Negotiating Rates".)

Inform all of your referral sources that you offer this, and make sure your marketing materials have something like: "sliding scale fees available, if necessary" or "a small percentage of my practice is dedicated to sliding scale cases". I recommend removing those statements from your marketing materials after you have a significant number of clients paying your regular rate or close to it. If you receive a new client at a sliding scale fee that is quite low and barely worth it for you, I would suggest getting full payment in cash before each session begins. Otherwise, you will risk not getting enough for yourself. Also remember that just because someone does not have coverage to see you, it does not mean you should jump straight to sliding scale. After all, sliding scale is for people without coverage <u>and</u> without a lot of income. I have had many cases in my practice where the client did not have coverage but did have more than enough money to pay our fee and then some! For example, think about all the people who are self-employed and do not have mental health coverage or have an HMO with very limited coverage. These people may actually have huge income sources, so there is absolutely no need to offer sliding scale and have them take your "limited" sliding scale spots from people that truly need it. Regardless, I have found that a sliding scale case, when the client is able to pay the agreed-upon fee without much of a problem, is much easier than dealing with a third party payer and client copays. In addition, they can give you useful knowledge and experience which you can build upon, increasing your feelings of confidence when you try to build self-pay full-fee clientele.

Some additional advice about low fee cases: I have been in situations, in the past, where clients made mistakes and told others about the rate they were paying to see me. If someone calls and quotes a certain low rate that she was told you would take, if you are unable to take another case at that rate, feel free to say that you cannot take that rate for any new cases. After all, the fee was set in the past for a specific client and her financial issues, as well as her specific clinical case. The rate can also change as well, as it is not set in stone forever. Do not be afraid to make general statements like that, in order to protect yourself and your livelihood.

I would not recommend offering a free consultation as this just has not really worked well for us. Most clients expect to be able to ask questions before making an appointment anyway, and every professional I know allows questions to be asked before an appointment is made.

COLLECT TESTIMONIALS

If you are doing your job and serving clients well, you will be able to collect testimonials. If one or two clients do not openly offer a testimonial, they will surely give you information that you can easily turn into one. When someone gives you positive feedback, ask her if she would be willing to write it down for you, just a few sentences, for your marketing materials. You can let her know you will not attach her name to it, as it will be completely anonymous. Then take the testimonial, verbatim, and place it on your marketing materials. You can have a "testimonials" page, or section. I would recommend keeping them concise. Remember, you want to keep the viewer's attention. But a few of these can give you more credibility and also can give the reader a better idea about what you can offer.

I think testimonials are important to do especially if you have a consulting, coaching, or training piece to your business. You could give all satisfied clients a brief survey at the end of their services to see what types of positive feedback they have. On this survey, you can ask if their feedback can be placed on your website with their identifying information removed. Thus far I have only done testimonials with consultation clients. I think it works quite well with consulting, coaching, or training clients, and possibly medical clients, but I would still remove their full names, and would also keep this page brief, with something like "Here are what a few of our clients had to say" at the top.

No client base yet? Consider offering low-fee services in exchange for feedback. Then, when you obtain positive reviews, ask if you can use them in your marketing materials, without their names attached, of course.

CONSIDER TAKING MANDATED CLIENTS

Mandated cases have their definite pros and cons. The pros are that you do not have to sell yourself to the client (because they will be required to see you), and they usually show up for their sessions. You will usually get paid, and closer to your regular fee. You may also be able to charge for some extras such as paperwork, telephone conversations, and letter-writing. In addition, with mandated clients, you do not always have to deal with insurance companies for payment. The other positive is that you can frequently get mandated clients to come in during daytime hours (which is usually preferable anyway, given some of these situations).

The negative side of this type of work is that the cases do not always turn out positive. When this happens, you have to report a negative outcome, which can be risky and needs to be handled with "kit gloves". Mandated cases also seem to have a more urgent and time-consuming feel, which can be irritating to some. But, for the most part, working with mandated clients has been positive for us. We take supervisor-referred EAP cases, court-ordered anger management clients, and various mandated substance abuse referrals. We always make sure we fully understand what the client's expectations are, what the treatment requirements are, and the credentials that are necessary in the provider. So, we ask all of these questions, and make sure the client does as well, in order to make sure nothing falls through the cracks and there are no misunderstandings with any involved party.

GET YOUR PREVIOUS CLIENTS BACK WITH REACH-OUT LETTERS

If you have had some clients that have dropped out of treatment and you have not heard from them in a while, why not send them a brief letter? Reach-out letters have worked well in my practice and ethically it is a good thing to do. Having sent one can also make you look much better if there ends up being some sort of dispute with the case. It is also much easier and less expensive to get previous clients back than to start with all new clients anyway.

Have a general reach-out letter template on file, and then tailor it a bit to each specific client. Stay brief, positive, professional and objective, with statements such as "I have been trying to contact you to schedule our next appointment but have been unable to reach you... please contact me if I can be of any further assistance... I hope you are doing well... Just so you know, if I do not hear from you within one month of this letter, I will be closing the chart... ", and then include all of your contact information. Make sure it is positive, inviting, and professional, and that you come across like you would be glad to hear from them. Use your letterhead for these and enclose a business card or two. For confidentiality reasons, make sure each letter is sealed well and is in a privacy envelope addressed to the right person. If you have permission to communicate with the client via e-mail, then these can also be sent that way.

These can work especially well with EAP clients who have additional free sessions to use. In these types of cases, it is quite helpful to give a reminder to clients that have "x" amount of free sessions remaining.

Sometimes, sending reach-out letters can actually result in clients contacting us to say how much we have helped them and that they are doing well. We like those types of messages, don't we? It also does not hurt that with these letters, they have our contact information in front of them yet again, so they can easily use it in the future if needed or pass it along to others.

JUST ASK!

Everyone can be a referral source or assist in some way, so just ask. Ask your satisfied clients, referral sources, other professionals, friends, family, and so on. There are many ways to subtly do this and not sound desperate. In addition, do you see any lists you would like to be included on? If so, just ask how your practice can be added. You will be surprised how many times lists (that will be seen by many) are free or very low cost to join (especially if you come across as a helpful service to the community). Also, if there is a website you belong to that features "Counselor of the Month", ask to be showcased in the next available month. So, always be aware of your surroundings and possibilities, and do not assume you will be turned down for anything, or any idea. As far as your satisfied clients go, I would think most will be quite happy to pass along your information as the professional with "very helpful service".

GIVE YOUR CARDS TO CLIENTS THAT HAVE SUCCESSFULLY COMPLETED TREATMENT

Make sure that all of your previously treated and satisfied clients have your business cards. Give your cards to these clients along with brief messages such as "I really enjoyed working with you", "My door is always open in the future", and "I just love getting referrals".

CREATE PRODUCTS RELATED TO YOUR SPECIALTIES

Writing a book, e-book (online), workbook, or booklet can increase your credibility and exposure. It can also produce additional passive income, creating another "income stream". In addition to traditional publishing, self and on-demand publishing are options which allow you to publish quickly and control the content and style of your work. You can also create DVDs or CDs, with a bit of technical assistance. When selling items on your website, be sure to put a "Buy Now" button on your home page and list a customer service phone number.

I have also recently seen opportunities for therapists to write for online CEU organizations. They may be referred to as "course contributors" or "contributing authors". With these opportunities, you can add "income streams", increase credibility, and build recognition.

HAVE PROMOTIONAL ITEMS MADE

Have promotional items made such as pens, "stress balls", or organic seed packets. Although this is not the least expensive route, consider having some fun things made with your practice name and contact information on them. Do your research to find the best deals. Then distribute to all of your referral sources and colleagues. Also, pass them out at seminars, events, or booths you may by "manning". Consider having the items in your waiting area for clients to see and pick up. Be careful of food products, though, due to the increasing number of people with food allergies and intolerances.

It is a good idea to have pads of paper or paper cubes in your session room with your name and credentials printed on them. When you are writing down recommendations for clients (or they are writing something for themselves), the paper will always include your information.

You can also create "how-to" sheets. One idea might be on a topic such as "How to Get a Good Night's Sleep". Include your name, credentials, and contact information. Then make them available and distribute them to everyone you know, in every way possible.

PARTICIPATE IN A BUSINESS OR HEALTH FAIR

Personally, I have not tried setting up a booth at any kind of fair (besides health fairs representing EAPs), so I cannot speak on whether or not that would be fruitful for you. It would seem that it would take a great deal of time and money setting it all up, having some items to display and distribute, sitting at the booth for hours talking to people, then being involved in the take-down process. This may get you a few clients, or it may not. You may wish to take a chance on a fair that seems right for you. If it ends up being worth it in the long run and you do not mind the work, then by all means keep doing it!

Do you have an opportunity to set up a booth at a business fair of some sort? If so, then have an interesting poster and banner for people to look at, as well as items they can take home. Of course you will display your brochures and business cards. Having hand-outs on less "stigmatized" topics such as stress or insomnia will help. You may also want to have brochures on topics such as "What is Hypnosis?" Having a bowl of wrapped healthy snacks may also make you stand out and attract people to your booth (stay away from peanut products, due to the growing number of people with peanut allergies). Having "Stress Dots" or some other similar activity will make your booth memorable. Distributing your "fun" promotional items at your booth will be necessary. The more interesting and entertaining your items are, the more you will attract people to your business.

SEEK ORGANIZATIONS THAT LINK PEOPLE TO WELLNESS PRACTITIONERS

There are some new and unique organizations that are creating ways for people to access alternative health and wellness providers, and services that may not be covered by insurance. Some of these organizations are contacting employers to provide membership cards for employees, which entitle them to discounted services from provider members. There is no middle man, and no one to approve or deny sessions. Instead, providers agree to offer their services at a discount to members. From what I have seen, there is sometimes a fee to become a provider, however this usually includes a listing in their directories which is an added bonus. Similar lists or organizations may also be found by including terms such as "guilds", "alternative healthcare provider lists", and "health savings cards" into your searches.

CONSIDER RADIO OR TELEVISION

Radio or television advertising are not usually low cost methods, but they might bring you many self-pay and full-fee clients quite quickly. If you have some money to spend, think you have something special to offer, and can craft a well-done strategic commercial, give it a try! Along these lines, I was just invited by a talk radio station to host a talk show on holistic therapy. This type of situation may be an option for those wishing to have that type of exposure. There is no reason that you cannot contact talk show producers to see if they need an expert for an upcoming program. Even if they say no, they can keep your name on file for any future needs. Many of us have been contacted (unsolicited) by programs (we have three times!), so establishing some relationships can only increase your odds of being asked to participate in a program in some way.

When I was growing up, my mom worked as a counselor in a hospital. I remember once listening to her being interviewed about her work by a local radio station. She was contacted by them to provide the interview. Therefore, I have faith that most of you can create a situation like that for yourself as well!

LOOK INTO NEWSPAPER OR MAGAZINE ADVERTISEMENTS

Research what might be available as far as newspaper and magazine ads. You might find a really good deal somewhere on low-cost ads or possibly an opportunity to place free ads (I have seen this occasionally). I would not recommend paying a lot for newspaper or magazine ads. Some say that "You have to just make sure it runs long enough so it finally reaches someone who wants to call or at least clip out your information". That may be so. I have not done too much of this, but what I have done did not yield many results. A counselor who worked in my practice wrote articles for a popular local paper on a monthly basis and she received quite a few referrals from this. But this was done every month, where she got paid and also had her contact information on the bottom of each article. So, I think articles can get some results if the topics are common, if articles run regularly, and they are done in a popular paper or magazine. I would just stay away from running expensive newspaper or magazine advertisements for now.

If you decide to go this route, or you find a good opportunity, then I recommend doing "target marketing" where you place your ad in a publication that focuses on your target market. For example, if you are into holistic methods, you may want to place an ad in a magazine focused on healthy living. Mass marketing, such as placing ads in general-interest papers and magazines, will probably yield limited results, unless run for a long period of time. Due to the high cost of some of these ads, it may not be an economical choice because of the small percentage of readers who may be in the market for your services. You can improve your chances for success by placing ads in publications with a target market closer to your own.

CONSIDER DIRECT MARKETING

Direct e-mail marketing can be a fruitful method if you intend to market your services to other professionals or business owners. I do not recommend that you send "cold" e-mails to prospective mental health clients with whom you have had no prior contact, however. Make sure any marketing e-mails are brief and explain quickly how your product or service can help the recipient. Include a professional brochure in an attachment if possible. Also make sure each e-mail is tailored specifically to the recipient as much as possible, using their name and such.

I have not tried sending direct mail to potential therapy clients. Some of my consultation clients had tried this in the past, and had gotten very poor results, especially considering the significant amount of time and expense involved in this method.

I have not tried sending out newsletters, or that type of e-mail marketing, so I cannot speak on whether or not it is worth it. It seems like they would be quite a bit of work and the people receiving them likely already know about you. But, there are newsletter services for a fee where you would not have to do much work (like ready-made newsletters) and they can be sent via e-mail to those that have signed up to receive them. You could have your website visitors sign up for newsletters if they wish, and can also have "sign up boxes" in your waiting areas for clients. It seems you can include announcements and specials/coupons for your business on each newsletter which can be beneficial. But, if you are interested in doing this, I would do some online research and would also ask around to at least two other professionals that do newsletters to see if they think this method is fruitful. If you decide you would like to try this, then I suggest sending them to people who know you, your clients, your former clients, and current referral sources. It would also be necessary to give recipients a clear and easy "opt out" at the end of each newsletter in case they would rather not receive any additional mail or e-mails in the future. I would also recommend that you send them very infrequently and make sure they are truly educational.

INVEST IN A FAX MACHINE/COPIER/SCANNER

You will use office machines more that you realize! They will save time and money and will help with marketing and billing. You will also get more EAP referrals this way, because the referral case managers will usually want to fax the authorizations for cases, and if you do not have a fax, the next counselor on the list who does have a fax may get the case over you.

CHECK EVERY LIST

One theme that is obvious thus far is that you will need to be on lists! This is the best way to grow your practice. Therefore, since this is so important, check every list you are supposed to be on to make sure it is 100% complete and accurate. This means all internet listings, insurance/EAP panels, resource lists, and so forth. Make sure your name and credentials are accurate as well as all your demographic and contact information (including all of your locations). Also make sure you are easily found in searches on each site. As mentioned earlier, it would surprise you to know how many times I found my provider information to be incomplete or inaccurate with various insurance and EAP companies. These lists are frequently what potential clients, as well as referral sources, are using for their searches. There also have been mistakes in some of my online listings. I have seen both incorrect information as well difficulty within the site searching for my name (such as my name does not come up even though I have typed in my demographics or services provided). There have also been times when my name was not added to a list as promised. You <u>will</u> lose out on potential business if these types of mistakes or omissions are not corrected, and many times it will need to be <u>you</u> correcting their problem, mistake, or omission. Be sure to make this an ongoing marketing task.

Perseverance is not a long race; it is many short races, one after another.

~ Walter Elliot

Chapter Two

Making the Sale

Afer implementing most of the marketing methods in Chapter One, you will surely have a potential client on the phone! Your confidence will be building as well. This chapter gives several tips for turning a simple inquiry into a client.

LET THEM KNOW THEY ARE CALLING THE RIGHT PLACE

Make sure callers know they are contacting the right type of organization. If they are calling you, you will usually have something they need, so make sure they know this. If they sound unsure about whether they have called the correct place, ask them what they are looking for, and then assure them they are contacting the correct type of organization. Of course there will be situations where they need to contact a different place, but more often than not, you will have services they need.

Suppose the caller says "I'm looking for someone for depression", then your response could be something like "Yes, we work with depression... I think we can really help... We do counseling and psychotherapy, and depression is something we specialize in". Assure them that you can help, at least initially.

Of course we do not ever want to word it like we have a magic wand and can cure everything, but make it sound like there are definite things they can gain from coming in to see you. Again sounding competent, kind, respectful, and at the same time trying to make some kind of connection with the client.

Ask: "Did you have an insurance plan you wanted to use?" Then, if you are in-network for their insurance or EAP, make sure they know. You may word it like "Yes we take that insurance, we're in-network, so it should be fine". Notice I said "should" because with insurance it might not be fine, but if it looks good, inform clients of that. That is a great connector or ice breaker if you are saying "we're in-network". It is almost like an instant "in", especially if there are few others in-network.

If you are proud of your website and you have gotten referrals and positive feedback from it, provide the address to clients if it may help make the sale. With your website, clients can get more information that can assure them you can help.

Many professionals are frequently asked, "What is your specialty?" When faced with this question, I would first ask what they are looking for and then speak to that. I would briefly explain how you see therapy and symptoms, as well as your approaches to treatment. If you think you can help with their problems, inform them of that, and in what ways. If you have had specific experience or training in what they want help with, be sure to mention that as well. If it is a referral source on the line, then the same things apply, but you will be thinking more about how you can make the caller know he needs you.

Think about how you can communicate the fact that you can make his job easier and fill a need for him. You will want to communicate all those aspects to referral sources and they will love you for it, trust me!

Practice all of your potential spiels! Having "phone scripts" will lead to self-confidence. It is also courteous because it helps keep the conversation brief, an important consideration when speaking to a busy person. Set up pretend conversations with people you trust so you can practice what you will say and how you will say it. Welcome honest feedback from them. Be sure to see Chapters Three and Four for tips on how to discuss your fee, so you will be prepared on how to discuss that.

So you will want to communicate to potential clients that they have called the right place, make a connection quickly with them, and come across as experienced, knowledgeable, competent, and kind.

BE UNIQUE

Tell the caller what makes your practice stand out, during the first conversation. Treat this like your one minute commercial. This is often called an "elevator speech". If all you had was the length of an elevator ride to clearly explain your services and how you stand out from the competition, what would you say? Write a list of positive attributes where you differ from most other professionals in your area. Include on this list all of the ways your practice is efficient and effective. Your success stories, tailored to specific concerns, will also be quite useful here. Keep this "elevator speech" with you to refer to during these interactions. Spend some time developing this brief overview and remember to keep it positive.

BE POSITIVE

Smile and think positive thoughts. Clients will sense that on the phone, or over e-mail communications, and may respond more favorably to you. Make a positive statement about yourself during the first call. For example, you can say something like, "I am very accommodating and will stay open extended hours if necessary."

The more experience and success stories you have, the easier it will become to be positive and truly believe that the client is better off with you than with another professional. Your clients, the ones who like you, will help you deepen your belief system, to a point where it becomes impenetrable.

Our doubts are traitors, and make us lose the good we oft might win, by fearing to attempt.

~ William Shakespeare

TAKE AN INTEREST IN THE CLIENT'S TOWN

Take an interest in the client's town, or in the very least, know where it is! I recommend having a copy of a map with all of your intake materials, so when you have a potential client on the line, you can at least tell him you know where his town is. You can say something like "Oh yes, that is just two towns over from our office". It will sound intelligent and inviting to the potential client. In session you can also talk briefly about his town and what positive things you know about it. This will make you sound informed, intelligent, and interested in him as a person. Clients like that!

BE DIVERSE IN YOUR APPROACHES

Having specialties and niche marketing is smart, but you will also have to be somewhat diversified in your techniques or approaches in order to succeed in private practice. For example, offering just art therapy alone will not get you a full caseload. But, providing a large menu of techniques to choose from such as art and expressive therapy, CBT, psychodynamic, and relaxation techniques will probably get you a full private practice caseload. You can still do some art therapy and market yourself as incorporating that technique into your treatment sessions when appropriate, but you cannot focus solely on a very narrow specialty and expect to succeed in private practice. I just do not think that would work in this setting.

PROMPTLY RETURN CALLS AND E-MAILS TO POTENTIAL CLIENTS AND REFERRAL SOURCES

You can definitely "win" referrals by being responsive, this I know for sure. Some clients or referral sources call around to the first therapist who picks up the phone or returns their inquiry. If you are the first, then you might get the sale over someone else. You will also give the impression that you will be very responsive to their needs during the therapy, which is the message you will want to be giving when trying to build your practice.

OFFER TO BILL THE CLIENT'S INSURANCE

Obviously if you are in-network for the client's insurance, your practice will likely be doing the insurance billing for the client, but not all clients know that, so tell them. Also, if you are out-of-network for their insurance and you think they might have some coverage with you (due to having a PPO or something similar) inform them of that and then consider telling them you will bill their insurance for them. This may win you more clients. It certainly won't hurt. You will have to make certain of all of their benefits first, and how their insurance works, before you charge anything else but your full rate upfront, but this can work out well. It just might take a little time to figure out at first and might take some adjusting until you get to know their particular insurance, how it works, and what it pays. Anyhow, when I have a potential client on the line and it is in-network insurance, I usually inform him that we will do his insurance billing for him. Who wouldn't like to hear that?

Dealing with insurance companies can be stressful for clients, so anything you can do to ease this stress will help you make the sale with potential clients. Explaining how the insurance billing will work certainly helps.

CREDIT CARDS CAN HELP

If you decide to take credit cards, mentioning that can help make the sale. It can be particularly useful with self-pay or superbill clients who are having "cash flow" problems. With superbill clients specifically (clients who submit their own insurance bills), often they obtain their insurance reimbursement before actually having to pay their credit card bill! This is something of course you do not want to promise to a client, but you would definitely want to mention it. In addition, sometimes clients like using credit cards just for the convenience of it, but also due to what they may receive in return, such as frequent flyer miles or points they can use to buy products or services.

WHEN AN EAP CALLS WITH A POSSIBLE REFERRAL...

When an EAP contacts you with questions about a possible referral, and you want to take EAP cases, you are going to want to communicate quickly that you can take the case right away, that you have the correct specialties, and possibly that you are in-network for the client's insurance (if that is known). If it is apparent that you are not in-network for the client's insurance, you can communicate that you will make very efficient use of all EAP sessions (as always), and then will be willing to "work with" the client on fee reductions as well as help them access any out-of-network coverage.

ONE-TIME AGREEMENTS ARE POSSIBLE

If a potential client would have no coverage to see you and has no ability to self-pay, you can have the client contact his benefit plan to see if a "one-time agreement" can be done. This agreement would allow the client to see you under his in-network coverage. You would also have to negotiate a rate with the plan. Make sure you are comfortable with the rate as well as all other possible requirements. "One-time agreements" happen occasionally, especially in cases where the area provider or affiliate network is limited or you offer something rare that the client needs. Therefore, if a potential client contacts you and has an EAP or limited insurance plan which you are out-of-network for, there may still be some options for coverage.

TURN DISCOUNT REQUESTS INTO OPPORTUNITIES

Has a client ever said something such as "Your fee is too high and I'd like a discount"? What if you say "yes" and immediately drop your fee. Then the client might think one of the following: you seem desperate; your rate could have been lowered even more; your original rate was not real; you do not value your work; it is possible to get a discount again in the future. The problem with quickly giving a discount is that you have given away something and have asked for nothing in return, possibly creating a win-lose situation. The client has "won" a discount and you have "lost" it. Also, just because you have agreed to a lower fee does not mean you will get the case. Instead of giving the immediate discount, kindly ask for more information. Asking why they need a discount will help you understand what is behind the request. Then, depending on the response, you could use different approaches.

One approach can be useful if money really is limited. Instead of giving a straight discount, you lower the "rate" by removing something of value. This is a win-win situation. Maybe offer some suggestions, such as it would need to be a daytime appointment, "cash only", or shorter sessions for that rate. It is a good idea for your clients to understand that there is some kind of price for reducing the rate.

Another approach could be useful if money is not limited. With this approach, you agree to give a discount as long as they give you something in return. In exchange for a discount you ask them to give you something which is of value to you. This is another win-win situation. For example, suppose you provide consulting at $150 an hour, and someone asks for a discount. You could say, "I am prepared to reduce my rate from $150 to $130 an hour if you agree on two additional hours of consultation time." The client will receive the discount and you have received a commitment for two additional hours. This is another win-win situation. (Also see Chapter Four, under section "Bulk Payments Can Be Win-Win").

If you are dealing with a discount request from a company such as an EAP, on a task such as a seminar, see if they can throw in extras such as travel time reimbursement and authorizing a longer amount of time on-site. Also request that you be called first, for the next onsite tasks, in return for the discount.

So, I hope you see that when potential clients ask for discounts, it actually creates opportunities for you. Whatever you do, it is a good idea for it to be a win-win situation for both sides and that the client is perfectly clear as to why you are lowering your fee. I believe there should always be a good reason to give a discount. Depending on the way you respond to these types of requests, you can end up with a much bigger "sale".

See Chapters Three and Four for more advice on how to discuss payments and set appropriate rates. Also see Chapter Five ("Attracting Your Ideal Client") for additional advice on making the sale with your "ideal clients".

Chapter Three:

Spending Too Much Time for Too Little Money?

This chapter will go over all of the time-saving tips I have learned throughout the years I have been working as a professional. It will also give advice on how to save money and increase your bottom line at the same time.

KEEP VARIOUS COSTS DOWN

Search for free or low cost services for yourself (such as Continuing Education Unit opportunities) and keep them on file for when they are needed. As noted earlier, major professional associations often offer free CEUs. There is also a website that offers free CEUs to social workers. At least in Illinois, I believe social workers can obtain all of their CEU hours online, so that can be a huge money saver.

Negotiate with advertising, marketing, and listing sources to keep those fees as low as possible (also see Chapter One for free and low cost marketing methods).

Do whatever you can to lower your phone bill and charges. Decrease to just the basic services you need and nothing more. If you continually do not use all of your "minutes", then decrease your package.

Negotiate or re-negotiate your office rent. See if you can pay lower rent than what the office is priced at. If you are already in a lease, when it is up for renewal, you can request lower rent or request that your rent not increase. This will be much easier if you are seen as a good tenant who always pays on time. Let them know that it would be difficult for you to pay the amount they are asking, and then see what happens! I have seen this to be especially fruitful in hard economic times, as well as when an office building is not currently full of tenants. Use supply and demand to your advantage whenever you see an opportunity!

There are also organizations that allow clinicians to bill insurance companies online for free! The only charge is to the insurance company.

Continually look over your business checking account ledger and credit card charge history to see if there are any unnecessary expenditures. Are there expenses that are not really helping your business which you can eliminate altogether?

CONSIDER SUBLETTING OFFICE SPACE

Subletting can be a great savings and an excellent way to increase the bottom line of your business. I would recommend that you either sublet your office space or rent out some of your space, at least initially, for at least one of your offices. Of course if you are subletting out, you will have to make sure it is okay with your building management first. You will also have to make sure that the days you will be giving away will not inconvenience you or your clients in any way, because then it might not be worth it. If subletting someone else's space, it is a good idea for the office to fit with your personality and is comfortable for you and your clients. Also make sure that the days available will be good for you and your clients in that area. In addition, it is important that you will get along well with the people you are renting from (or to) and sharing space with (and maybe you will give referrals to each other!). One other word of caution when subletting someone else's office is that you may not look official or established enough. Therefore, it is highly recommended that you place your name plate (with credentials) on the office door (for at least the days you use the office). You are going to need to make sure you have a name plate everywhere you possibly can have one, as well as have your framed license displayed in your session room. Do whatever you can to make sure your name and credentials get added to any building directories as well. Your business cards (along with brochures, if at all possible) will need to be in the waiting area. Last but not least, negotiate the office rent to make it a better situation for you! Negotiate, negotiate, negotiate!

USE THE SUPERBILL RECEIPT

For health professionals, using the superbill method for out-of-network insurance billing will not only save time and money, but the payment for services is upfront, in most cases, from the client/patient. The superbill is a receipt you can give to the client that they can later use to submit to their insurance for re-imbursement. Like I said earlier, if you stand out in the crowd of professionals, the client is connected with you, and is able to pay upfront, this should not be much of a problem. In some cases you may have to decrease

nal rate a bit in order to "make the sale" with a self-pay/superbill client, but it is not always necessary. When you have worked on increasing your skills in certain areas of interest, you will be looking very desirable to many potential clients. Also, when you have worked a while on your internet marketing, you will eventually start seeing some quality referrals coming from that as well.

A basic superbill receipt contains the following, but depends on the specific insurance requirements:

Patient's full formal name (as registered under the insurance)

Patient's date of birth

Diagnosis

Dates of service and CPT codes

Amounts charged to patient with total on bottom

Amount paid by patient along with "Balance Due: Zero" "Paid in Full"

Provider's full name, credentials, contact information, practice name

Provider's tax ID # (usually needed) (not your social security #)

Patient's insurance ID # and policy # (sometimes these are needed)

You may want your superbill receipts made into forms that create instant copies. Since this is somewhat expensive to do, make sure you are happy with your forms first, before you submit for printing.

Do not give superbill receipts to clients for sessions if they have not paid the full agreed-upon rate yet. The reason is that if they have not paid you yet, they could end up getting "reimbursed" by their insurance, but not pay you. The insurance will not help you out with this type of situation. You will be on your own! It is best to just give a regular basic receipt if the client only partially paid, then let them know you will give them the insurance reimbursement receipt once it is paid in full.

Important note about a new law affecting HMOs: I have read recently that there is a new law that was passed requiring HMOs in Illinois to partially reimburse some patients for services rendered by out-of-network mental health professionals. I do not know the details of this new law, when it goes into effect, or what other states are affected. But it just goes to show that patients should fully educate themselves on their benefits, and get informed of any updates in their plans as they come. You may want suggest, to your out-of-network HMO clients, that they submit a superbill receipt or two, periodically, to see if there will be any coverage.

Note that there are a few PPO-type plans that require out-of-network pre-authorization before releasing any out-of-network benefits to the patient. Situations like this are just another reason clients should know their benefits inside and out.

INSURANCE BILLING ADVICE AND TIPS FOR MENTAL HEALTH PROFESSIONALS

Many clinicians do not know that family psychotherapy sessions typically reimburse more than individual sessions when submitted to insurance. Therefore, if the client has coverage for family sessions, consider billing "family" whenever possible (when a family member has been involved in the session during a client appointment, it can usually be considered "family", but check with the insurance companies you are involved with first). Now, there are a few insurances that pay the same for family sessions, and there are one or two that may pay a little less for family sessions. So it would be wise to look into your contracts, and also make sure the client has this type of coverage first.

If you contact the insurance about this coverage, make sure you word it exactly like this "Does the patient have coverage for family sessions, family treatment". If you do not word it like this they may think you are asking about "family coverage", which is different. If an authorization is needed then make sure the family CPT code is included in the auth. You may also want to try billing "family" once for a particular client, to see how it works out, before continuing to bill "family". But, most of the time I have found that family treatment is covered, or can be authorized, and gets reimbursed at a significantly higher rate for the same amount of time spent in session. I also think that knowing about the higher rate is important because cases that involve family are usually more time-consuming as a whole, so you will need to collect everything that you have a right to collect.

Double sessions can often be paid by insurance. I have seen many times, with some major insurance companies, that two sessions (or two units) in one day can be paid. This frequently involves cases where family treatment is being done, and we bill one individual and one family session in one day, under the same client (or one evaluation and one follow-up individual or family session). Remember, "per session" copays usually still apply. Thus far, billing double sessions has worked out quite well for us for the most part. Sessions are about an hour and a half (two 45-minute sessions), and they need to be different CPT billing codes otherwise the second one might be seen as duplicate billing with some insurance companies (unless a modifier is added). Of course the client needs to have the coverage for this, both in the CPT codes billed as well as the number of sessions allowed per day/week/year. Managed care and EAP companies probably will not allow double sessions, but you can double check. Sometimes they only allow (or authorize) one session per week, but that would need to be confirmed with each specific company. Also if the client is in crisis, the insurance, managed care company, or EAP may make an exception due to the situation.   After all, their major goal is to prevent any kind of hospitalization, because it is extremely expensive.   So, if authorizing a double session or two sessions per week might prevent disaster, then they very well might do that.

Longer therapy sessions might be covered for a client, and may pay at a higher rate by the insurance.   Lately we have billed the CPT code 90808 to a major insurance company and it has been paid, and at a considerably higher rate than shorter sessions.   A 90808 is a 75-80 minute follow-up psychotherapy session, and we have used it for cases where we are doing EMDR (Eye Movement Desensitization and Reprocessing) and need the extra session time. One of my counselors discovered this after attending EMDR training and then she contacted our main insurance contract to see if they would honor this. They said they would and it has worked out well thus far.   Just make sure it is covered by the client's plan, it is medically necessary, and it is included in the pre-authorization if that is needed.   Also, the client copay/coinsurance will probably be higher, especially if it is based on a percentage of the rate. In addition, the amount applied to a deductible will probably be higher as well.

Evaluations typically reimburse higher than follow-ups, and sometimes quite a bit higher! A word of caution: There are a few plans out there where the evaluation pays slightly lower than follow-ups, so you will again have to check your contracts.   But, what I have learned through the years is that you can bill a psychotherapy evaluation again if you have not seen the client in a while!   I think for most, the magic window is three months.   Again, you will want to check and see with your specific contracts, their rates and policies, but I have found this to be the case with most insurance contracts I have worked with.   If there needs to be an auth in place, make sure they include all the correct (and possible) CPT codes you may be using with a case.   But think of all the extra compensation you could receive just knowing this!

Note that if you bill an insurance company less than the contracted rate, or allowed amount for that service, you will get paid less than your contracted rate or allowed amount. For example, if the evaluation rate with an in-network insurance company is $124 and you bill $90, then they will apply $90 to the benefits. You will get paid from the $90 charge even though $124 would have been allowed.

Finally, to simplify things in your practice, I highly recommend doing your insurance billing online whenever you have the opportunity. This will save you a great deal of time and resources, in most cases.

BRING SOMETHING TO DO WHILE ON HOLD

Before calling an insurance company or organization where you know you will be on hold, bring work to do! You will have to accept the fact that you will be on hold sometimes, so take that as an opportunity to get other tasks done at the same time.

HAVE A MISSED APPOINTMENT POLICY

It is important to have a clearly written cancellation policy and frequently remind clients that it exists. Almost every therapist I know has a cancellation policy, so it should be nothing new to clients these days. In addition to having all new clients sign your policy, you can also display it in your offices as well as have it printed on the back of your business cards. You can even post it on your website. Feel free to kindly inform brand new clients of your policy, <u>before</u> their first appointment. The policy would not yet technically be enforceable for their first session without a signature, but you can still tell them you have a cancellation policy anyway! It is helpful to kindly explain to clients the reasons for the policy such as "If therapists let every client no-show or late-cancel to scheduled appointments without paying anything, they would go out of business. In addition, a whole hour is set aside especially for you and cannot be filled by another client late-notice. It is also important, for your treatment, for it to be necessary to show up for sessions."

You will need to explain to all of your insurance clients that insurance usually does not cover missed appointments, therefore clients are directly responsible for any missed appointment fees, in full. With EAP clients, you will have to review the EAP affiliate manual or speak with the staff to see what is allowed for missed appointments. Some EAPs reimburse for missed appointments, some allow affiliates to follow their own cancellation policy (such as charging clients if they miss an appointment after they sign the policy), and there are a few EAPs that do not compensate for any missed appointments or allow affiliates to charge any no-show fees. When the EAP does not allow anything for missed appointments, I urge you to still inform clients that is not okay for them to miss scheduled appointments, and that they need to call as soon as they think they might not be able to make it. Give them your cards every time you schedule an appointment!

Some clients have special needs, such as a physical condition, where they may need a special agreement. For example I might need to change my missed appointment policy for a client that has a chronic physical illness. If I see that this client usually knows 4 hours prior to our appointment whether or not she can make it, then I may set up a "4 hour missed appointment policy" for her. So do this when needed, when it is also feasible for you. You may keep a good client this way, and save your own sanity as well.

If you get a late-cancelation because the client cannot come in, consider offering a phone session, since the client will be charged for the service anyway.

But do phone sessions only if you feel you can, because anything short of collecting your full cancellation fee will be a favor to the client.

Do not talk with the client in length on a "no-show" or "cancellation" phone call if they are not going to be paying anything. This would be encouraging missing appointments, not having to pay for them, and getting a free session out of it! Not to mention your need to keep your own sanity in the process! Of course there are exceptions to the rule such as a suicidal client situation, but I think you know the scenarios to which I am referring. Just pin them down to rescheduling the appointment if there will not be an actual phone session at that time.

TOO MUCH MANAGED CARE AND NOT ENOUGH TIME OR MONEY?

Contracting with managed care companies can be quite helpful in building your caseload in the beginning of your healthcare practice. But it can become quite time-consuming as well, on top of low rates and potential problems with billing. If you are a mental health professional and feel like you are drowning in managed care, the first thing you can do right away is make sure you are doing 45-50 minute therapy sessions, as opposed to full one hour sessions. After all, you are only required to spend 45-50 minutes with each client per most insurance company/EAP contracts and authorizations. The extra time you will have you can use on those treatment plans, paperwork, and phone calls. Then, as you follow the methods mentioned in this book, you will be able to start dropping any contracts that have given you the most headaches and the lowest pay. This will free up some time, and leave some prime spots in your schedule for other referrals that will be coming in (this will be happening as long as you are working the methods in this book!). You may choose to keep a few of these contracts ongoing, in order to serve a goal for you (such as to make sure your day hours stay booked, or to make sure your caseload stays at a "safe" level for you during slower times).

Also, as mentioned earlier, managed care and insurance rates are negotiable often times, and can be raised. See what can be done by contacting the provider relations representatives.

BEWARE OF THOSE SEEKING FREE ADVICE OR COUNSELING!

Most of us have had the lengthy e-mail or voice mail from a person requesting help and asking many questions. Your main goal in these types of situations is to quickly see if you can even assist this person, and then if you think you can help, set an appointment. For example, if someone e-mails you with a lengthy story about their marital issues, you might respond with something such as "Looks like you have a lot to talk about... I do marital and individual therapy and I think I can help... I'd like to sit down with you and further discuss this". This usually works well. It conveys that you think what they have to say is important, that you want to hear about it, and that you think you can help. It also gives the message to them about how important a full assessment is. In addition, it subtly gives a message that professionals need to get paid for services rendered! We do not usually give out free advice or recommendations in my practice. One reason is that we can be found responsible for recommending something to a person, even if we gave it for free. Another reason is that we really need to assess the situation and the person before we can give sound professional advice anyway. There is yet another reason and I think you can guess. Yes, it is our time, our very valuable time.

CONSIDER OPENING UP NEW CASES

Sometimes opening up an additional case will make your life, and income, much better! For example, if you are working with a client under an EAP and one of her family members is taking time with what seem to be individual issues, then have a new case opened up under that person's name and get some sessions authorized (if it is okay with the client/family). This can make your work much less stressful, and you will be paid what you should be getting for your work. You will also then be able to focus on each person, making it much easier and effective. You can also do this with managed care and insurance cases, if the person who would be considered the identified client is covered under the plan.

TREATMENT PLANS AND AUTHORIZATION REQUESTS TAKING UP YOUR TIME?

I know from my experience working in the EAP and managed care fields, that you can keep your responses to psychotherapy treatment plan requests short and to the point. Do not spend a lot of time on these, but do make sure you answer all the questions. They are going to scan for some key points including: the basic techniques that you are using (evidence-based treatment), efficient use of sessions, use of community and other resources, as well as diagnosis and supporting symptoms (they will mainly be looking for symptoms of depression and anxiety). So if they see techniques and interventions such as CBT, education, assertiveness training, "home therapy" assignments, linkage with support groups and educational resources, along with a covered diagnosis and symptoms that support the diagnosis, you will be fine. Use the wording that I have used, as they will like that as well. They are not looking for a book (nor should they get one), and they cannot read through or review so much information anyway. You will save a lot of time, make them happy, and preserve some client confidentiality all at the same time. If the reviewing case managers feel comfortable working with you and you are speaking their language, you might get more sessions authorized after each review.

PURCHASE FURNITURE AND DÉCOR AT A DISCOUNT

If you are a psychotherapist, I recommend getting your office furniture and décor at a discount. You can get furnishings and décor from discount or low price stores, resale and antique shops, garage sales, friends and relatives who may like to donate to the cause, and places that sell hotel furniture (when hotels redecorate, they sell furniture to certain re-sale organizations). Also check your local papers to see if there is anything good for sale.

Negotiate prices as well and find out how you can get discounts! For example, I know that most antique stores give a considerable discount if you pay with cash or check. Also if you are buying many items, most shops will consider a bulk discount. We also know about furniture stores that offer free financing, or no payments until a certain time.

Remember, this is also an area in which to ask for donations from your family and friends; I mean what better cause would there be? Try sending a mass e-mail or letter to everyone you know, letting them know you are starting a practice and what items you need. Let them know it will go to a worthy cause (as your practice will help many people). Also let them know that you can pick up the item(s) from them which will make it easy for them. If you have some money, then let them know that, as some people may want to sell certain items, at a good price, but still may want to get something for it.

Just make sure all of the items are pleasing to the eye, are clean, look good together in your office, and are relatively comfortable. Have someone you know, who is skilled at decorating, help you out. It is a good idea to make sure your office has soothing colors and pictures, and interesting things for clients (and you) to look at. You might find interesting low-cost items that also serve as conversation-starters, which is another bonus.

GET FREE ITEMS FOR YOUR WAITING ROOM

Many people do not know this, but you usually can get free health magazines and newsletters and your local health food store. You can even set up free health magazines to be sent to your office on an ongoing basis. Many areas also have complementary visitor's guides as well, which can be an interesting read. Antique stores also frequently have free area antique guides which you can also put in your office. Also check your local library for magazines they are giving away. In addition I have found free magazines near the exit door at my local grocery store. I have gotten free children's activity books at local garden centers and plant nurseries as well. You may also find gently used magazines at resale shops. Ask for donations of magazines and books (and CD's for that matter), from your family and friends. I do not know anyone who would not want to "recycle" items after they are done using them. It is the "green" thing to do and you will get free things from it! So keep your eyes peeled and your mind open and you will find many sources of free items for your office.

SHOP FOR SUPPLIES AT DISCOUNT STORES

You can get activities, books, and other supplies at your local dollar store. Many resale shops also have books that you can place in your waiting area or session room bookshelf. Be sure to affix your practice labels on them before placing in your waiting area as people tend to walk off with these types of items.

OFFICE APPEARANCE AND LOCATION ADVICE FOR PSYCHOTHERAPISTS

Some would say that if you are a gifted therapist all you need is a room with two folding chairs. If you are extremely gifted, then I agree somewhat with this statement. But I do think you will want clients to be comfortable as they will most likely return for more services if they are. I think a nicely decorated, neat looking office, in a decent building and location is all you need. I would caution you not to overspend on your rent or your furnishings/décor. Now, I do not mean your office can be a dump in a bad building and unsafe location, because that will not work. But I also think that if your office is in a very high-end building, with very expensive furniture, some clients may feel uncomfortable. They may feel intimidated or think "Is the money I'm paying for services all going towards high rent and furnishings?". You want them to think that their money is going towards you, your relationship, and your credentials. That is where the value truly is, and most clients sense that. As long as your office is comfortable and clean, you will be ok. My offices are "middle of the road". They are in nice suburbs, near downtowns, rivers and parks, but they do not have expensive furnishings or décor and are not in high-end buildings. The offices, however, are comfortable, safe, relaxing, and professional. To the best of my knowledge, I do not think we have had a client not return because the office was not upscale enough. We have a very high percentage of clients that return for more services after their first session.

MAKE SURE YOU CHOOSE A BUSINESS CREDIT CARD THAT PAYS YOU BACK

Be sure to get a business credit card that gives you points or some kind of bonuses that you will use. For example, from my business card charges, I get a gift card for a store that I shop at frequently, after a certain number of points are racked up. Also make sure the credit card company does not charge you unnecessary fees, and contest them if you ever see any fees on your statement. Let them know you have been a good card holder and that you do not agree with the fee being charged to you. Remind them that there are many other business credit cards out there for you to choose from and that you will be "shopping around" for other deals if they do not waive the fee.

TOO MANY CALLS IN BETWEEN SESSIONS?

Are you getting too many calls or e-mails in between sessions? If clients seem to need to have long conversations between sessions, turn them into session appointments, even if over the phone or online. You could say: "Sounds like you have a lot going on and many things to talk about... Do you want to have a session now, or perhaps you can come in soon?" You can also teach them to write down things they want to tell you, to discuss in the next session. With this method they will not feel like they will forget to tell you, it can also help them vent, and can hold them over until their next session. If the calls you are getting are for rescheduling appointments (one of my "pet peeves"!), then make it a bit difficult to reschedule, by letting them know your schedule is getting busy. The message will be that if they keep cancelling, they will likely not get an ideal time again, or may have to wait a while to get back in. If needed, you can also gently convey the message that you are quite busy with your business and do not have much extra time for things outside of client sessions.

ARE CLIENTS STICKING AROUND YOUR OFFICE?

Yes it happens, they have something important to tell you and it is nearing the end of session. Let them know that what they are saying sounds very important and "let's begin the next session talking about this… that will give us plenty of time to cover everything… when do you want to come back?". This acknowledges the fact that they have something important to say and will give them the opportunity to talk, just at a different time. You can also have them come up with one to three topics they feel are most important to discuss in session, and bring the list into each session. This can ensure that every topic can be discussed prior to the end of session. In addition, you can have some kind of ritual towards the end of all sessions that gives the message it is coming to an end. Whether it is a book or a card you reach for, or a certain activity you do at the end of every session, it will help give the subtle message that the scheduled time is nearing the end. Of course, you are also going to want a clock facing you as well as one that faces clients. This way, everyone will know when the session time is ending.

Along these lines, it is important to take care of anything business-related at the beginning of sessions. This way, you will have time to discuss the matter if needed, and you can keep all sessions ending on positive notes, which is preferred.

LATE-ARRIVING PSYCHOTHERAPY CLIENTS?

Do not stay late or disrupt your schedule because clients arrive late. Simply inform them that you cannot stay late and that the session will still go to the usual time as scheduled. You must do this especially if this is a pattern for certain clients. They need to know that if they are late, they lose time with you (a consequence for behavior). You will be much less stressed, and will get your time back, if you follow this.

HAVE CLIENTS ARRIVE EARLY

Have all new clients arrive 15 minutes early to their first appointment. Have a clipboard out with "new client" paperwork for them to read, sign, and fill out. These forms would include your "new client information" form which requests all demographic, contact, and insurance information. Then you have consent forms and your HIPPA privacy form (separate the signature page so you can use the same packet for other clients). You also will have your "Statement of Understanding" form for them to read and sign. Put a sticky note on the paperwork, with their first name only, so they know it is for them, but it stays more confidential. I recommend having all clients arrive at least five minutes early to all scheduled appointments, even follow-ups. They can wait in the waiting room and get comfortable until it is time to begin session.

MAKE APPOINTMENT CONFIRMATION CALLS WHEN NECESSARY

There may be certain clients that always need a reminder call for their appointments, and some other situations where you may want to make quick calls to make sure clients are coming in. On snowy days, holiday times, or days where your appointments are scattered throughout the day, you are probably going to want to make sure everyone is coming in, and at the time they originally scheduled, so that your time is not wasted. Just keep in mind that if you do reminder calls with a client, he will always expect that. So, if you skip the reminder call one time, he may not show up because he relies on that call!

HAVE A WEBSITE THAT WORKS FOR YOU

On your website, it is quite helpful to have a profile page on yourself and point potential clients towards that if they seem to have many questions about you. You can also have your office location and directions on your website. This will save you much time with new clients. This may also help them get to your office on time as well, because the directions will be correct. Also having a "Frequently Asked Questions" page is a time-saver with clients. I have also seen practice websites that will take a client's credit card for payment! The client can pay the counselor via their website which directs the client to a secure site to input the credit card payment. So think of all the ways your website can increase time efficiency.

DECREASE MAIL

Decrease unwanted repetitive junk mail from coming to you. Contact all of the junk mail pieces coming to you to see how you can get off of the mailing list. You can also do this with mass e-mails that you receive that you do not need. On the bottom of each e-mail there usually is a way to remove yourself from the mailing list. Doing this consistently will eventually free up a considerable amount of time and will simplify your life!

DEALING WITH TINY COPAYS?

Consider collecting copays in bulk from clients you know are returning. We have some clients that have a $7 copay, and although some money is better than none in most cases, it just sometimes seems like a waste of time. So, consider collecting small copays in bulk. It will save time and make things much easier for you and the client.

INCREASE THE MINIMUM CHARGE FOR CREDIT CARD TRANSACTIONS

Spending too much time processing credit cards? If so, then either add a "minimum" amount that can be charged per transaction, or increase the minimum you have already set. Right now I have a $40 minimum in my practice policy because it takes too much of my time and money processing the smaller charges. So, clients with low copays will have to pay with cash or check, unless they are coming in frequently or are paying their copays in bulk.

SETTING YOUR RATE

Are you unsure what your rate should be? If so, then I suggest you take the highest reimbursement rate from your insurance contracts, for the highest reimbursed CPT code (e.g., evaluation) and set your rate a bit higher than that. So for example, if your highest contracted rate is $123, then I suggest making your rate $125 or $130, if you are comfortable with that. Check to see what others in your area are charging as their regular rate. If you fall somewhere in the middle, then I think that is good, because you will then know it is a fair amount for both you and the client. Also, a word of advice: therapists with additional credentials (such as a substance abuse certification), typically can ask for more. Therapists that have specialties, such as seeing small children, also can justify a higher amount. So, take all of that into consideration when setting your rate, and use your set rate as a starting point for all of your negotiations as needed.

If you are having some trouble "making the sale" and you suspect it might be your rate, do not decrease your fee for regular clients if you have current clients that are paying your full fee. Rather, start making changes and upgrades to your services. Begin doing things such as taking credit cards so you can state that in your initial conversation and in marketing materials. You may also wish to add positive aspects, such as offering full hour sessions, when others in the area typically offer 45-50-minute sessions. You might also have to "play up" your credentials and also add to them, to "justify" the rate. If you are having trouble "making the sale" and you have no current clients paying your set rate, then consider lowering your rate a bit. Give that some time and if that still does not help, then implement the above ideas as well.

You may want to consider setting your rate a bit lower than the average-priced counselor in your area. This may attract some referrals just because of the fair rate. If you do this, I suggest then not lowering your fee for anyone new as it is already a fair rate (unless you want to do a few true sliding scale cases as a way to build your practice, or have the desire and ability give back to your community in that way). One other nice thing about this strategy (setting your rate a bit lower than average) is that you will not have to negotiate with clients.

I would not, however, suggest setting your fee the absolute lowest in your area because this may make you look like you do not have quality services. Remember some of this is psychological. It is also not fair to the other providers in your area who cannot afford to set their fees so low. You do not want to bring down what potential clients and referral sources will expect to pay for services in your area. I know this may seem unselfish, but it actually is not in the long run, as you look at the big picture as well as your own professional future.

GOOD THERAPY IS EXPENSIVE!

When potential clients say to me "therapy is expensive", I do not disagree with them, because in some ways it is good for them to expect the expense. Having clients speak in general terms about the expense of therapy is also beneficial because it does not single out my practice as "the expensive one"! Unless the client qualifies for community mental health (or true sliding-scale rates), then all therapists will be costly. When I tell my husband about general conversations I have with people about our fees, and how some people do not want to pay much, he chuckles and says "Don't they know it's expensive to sit down with a professional?". Then I think "Yes that's right, they should all know this shouldn't they?" I am a healthcare professional and it is costly to "sit down with me"!

Why is good therapy expensive? Well, I am sure all of you can come up with a long list of reasons, and I encourage you to do so. My initial "reason" list is as follows:

1) I have invested in a large amount of schooling and training for myself.
2) My practice makes efficient use of all session time and provides effective treatments.
3) I am putting forth a great deal of time, effort, and energy with each case I take.
4) I am taking a professional risk with each interaction on each case I am involved with.

5) My office space and contents are expensive.

6) Malpractice insurance and license renewal are costly.

7) Obtaining required CEUs, marketing, dealing with insurance companies, credit card processing, accounting, and tax preparation are expensive and time-consuming.

8) Extra paperwork and phone calls are time-consuming and are usually "unpaid".

9) Occasionally, I do not get paid for my services, therefore I have to compensate for that unfortunate fact.

I know you have some of your own items to add. Perhaps you have to pay for child care every time you see clients. Maybe you have to pay for your own health insurance. So, you can see how long this list can become. If, while writing your list, you begin to feel a bit angry, then I have done my job! Referring back to *your* "reasons" list will help you feel stronger when standing behind your rate.

DO NOT OFFER SLIDING SCALE IMMEDIATELY!

As mentioned earlier, you will need to remember that just because someone has no coverage to see you, it does not mean you should jump straight to "sliding scale". After all, sliding scale is for people without coverage <u>and</u> without a lot of income. I have had many cases in my practice where the client did not have coverage but <u>did</u> have more than enough money to pay our fee and then some! For example, think about all the people who are self-employed and do not have mental health coverage, or have an HMO with very limited coverage. These very people may well have huge income sources, so there is absolutely no need to offer true sliding scale rates to these people! So, inform the caller of your rate and if there does not seem to be a problem, then leave it at that!

RAISE YOUR RATE

If you have had a certain set rate for some time and truly feel that it might be too low, then by all means raise it! Some signs your rate might be too low are: you have a waiting list; you have gotten additional certifications; you have added new services; you have obtained upgraded office space; you are starting to feel short-changed; you cannot afford your own therapy or supervision; your competitors are charging more than you; your rate is less than some of your contracted rates or allowed amounts from insurance companies. Most clients will be fine with a bit of a rate raise and may even see this as a positive, giving more value to your services. There is also a certain mindset (and I tend to agree), that coming to therapy actually makes people prosper and make more money themselves. Remember, your treatment is valuable! Just make sure you give all of your current self-pay/superbill clients at least one month's notice on your rate change so they can prepare their budget.

USE ONLINE LISTING SITES THAT CHARGE A SMALL FEE

Some online listing sites can save you a great deal of time. If you do not have time to consistently market your practice using many of the other methods in Chapter One, as mentioned earlier you may consider using quality online sites that will list your practice for a fee. These sites might get you a bit more "traffic" than the free sites. But again, I do caution you to make sure the sites you are considering come up quickly on search engines and are easy for potential clients to navigate. Make sure you sift through the entire site to educate yourself on everything it can possibly do for you. You will also want to negotiate the rate down as far as possible, if this can be done. I would advise not to choose the most expensive listing service. In addition, I would caution you about listing services that already have countless names on them in your area as this may not turn into enough actual clients for you. But, if you have a fair-priced listing, and many "potentials" are viewing your page (and not so many other pages), it could mean a steady stream of quality referrals without much work or money coming from you. It is possible to find that type of situation. So, if you are pressed for time but <u>do</u> have some money to spend, then sign up for as many paid listings as possible and let them do the work for you.

SOME ADVICE ON MANDATED CASES

If you accept supervisory referrals from EAPs, I would recommend doing only 45 minutes with the client, and using the last few minutes to call the EAP to give an update on the case. What they are going to want to know after every session is basically the following:

- Did the client show up?
- Is the client cooperative and motivated for change?
- Any new recommendations?
- When is the next session?

If you will need more (or more frequent) sessions, you can get them from an EAP more easily if the case has been referred (or suggested) by a supervisor. You may also be able to get some reimbursement for case management activities in these types of situations. Remember, EAPs need *you* more than you need them in these types of situations!

With court mandated cases, let the clients know that you charge extra for court paperwork and letters, as well as extra phone conversations. Let them know what your fees are upfront. Also, do not give a "treatment completion letter" until you have been paid in full by the client.

FIND OUT ABOUT ALL OF YOUR POSSIBLE TAX DEDUCTIONS!

Everything related to your business can be tax deductible, possibly including bad debt (unpaid amounts). So take complete advantage of everything you are entitled to. Read up on any new information on what could be considered a tax deduction for you. I also suggest consulting with a tax accountant as well (or read articles and attend seminars conducted by tax accountants) in order to make sure you are getting the most out of your deductions.

I was just at a seminar and the speaker was talking about state tax credits. One that caught my eye specifically was "rural tax credits" for social workers. Along the same line, she was also talking about "loan forgiveness" for social workers. So, be sure to take advantage of any credit your state might offer.

BE CAREFUL OF SALESPEOPLE

When you begin doing well, people will start trying to sell things to you. Just be careful to not let them waste your time and do not let them sell you things you do not need. Do not fall for their sales tricks because there will be many, believe me. It amuses me when they try to play their tricks on me. But anyway, do not let them pressure you. Always feel free to say "No thank you, goodbye".

WRITE A LIST OF TIME-CONSUMING TASKS

List all the tasks that you feel are taking too much of your time. Then brainstorm, one by one, for ideas on how to be more efficient. You may even find that you can eliminate some tasks altogether!

The ability to simplify means to eliminate the unnecessary so that the necessary may speak.

~ Hans Hofmann

Chapter Four:

Having Trouble Getting Paid for Your Services?

Believe me, I have been in these difficult situations plenty of times! So, let's see, you have gotten clients and have had some sessions, but have not been paid for some of your work? These days when benefits get misquoted or are incomplete, provider networks are so confusing you do not even know if you are in-network, clients forget their payments, and personal checks get returned, it can add up to a big problem. I do feel your pain, but it does not have to always be like that and there are definite ways to improve your cash flow. This chapter contains those recommended methods.

FIND WAYS TO GET ACCURATE AND COMPLETE INSURANCE BENEFIT QUOTES

First of all, during an initial contact with an insurance client, when you have agreed he will be coming to a session and it looks like it will be in-network, have him contact his insurance to get a mental health outpatient (or whatever type of service it is) benefits quote. The 800# for mental health is usually on the back of each health insurance card. Make it very clear that clients are responsible for their copay amounts upfront. Kindly let them know it is payable in "cash, check or credit card", or however it may be payable to you. In my practice, we obtain benefit quotes as soon as possible, any way we can. Sometimes we call the insurance (and speak with a live person), and sometimes we give the client a form to fill out with all the specific questions to ask the insurance (again, a live person), including what their co-insurance amount might be. This is separate from copay and frequently they will just quote "no copay". Then later when you get the payment or EOB (Explanation of Benefits) you may find they have a 50% coinsurance that has been taken out! So, with in-network clients, we have them bring a completed "benefits check" form to the first or second session. We also have them complete it at the beginning of each calendar year, when there frequently are changes. The following is an example of an "outpatient mental health benefits worksheet", with some wording you may want to use on your own forms for initial and ongoing clients:

2010 Outpatient MH Benefits Worksheet

Patient Name: _____DOB: _____

Full name of health insurance company: _____

Circle: HMO POS PPO Other: _____

Insurance card phone #'s: _____

Changes to Insurance ID or policy #'s: _____

Changes to Subscriber info: _____

Is there a managed care company involved in the management of your OP MH benefits for 2010? Yes / No

If so, give the full name of the managed care company: _____

Is Gina Spielman, LCSW & Assoc. In-Net? Yes / No (Tax id # _____)

(We are Out-of-Net for: _____)

In-Net Co-pay: _____In-Net Co-insurance: _____

In-Net MH OP Deductible: Ind: _____ Fam: _____
Per cal year? Yes / No   Any met?: Yes / No   If so, dollar amt. met?: _____
Combines with medical? Yes / No

Number of In-Net Mental Health Outpatient sessions allowed per year: _____
Dollar Amt Limit: _____

Does your OP mental healthcare require precert?: Yes / No   If so, has it been precerted? Yes / No   What is the auth # including dates: _____
What is the phone # to call for auth?: _____

In-Net Mental Health Outpatient Claims Address: _____

At the first session, we at least ask the client if she knows what her copay or deductible amounts are for mental health outpatient. In the very least, look on the client's insurance card and see if there is any information on copay amounts. If there are any copays listed, then consider taking the higher one (usually "specialist" copay) until you have a clearer picture of what her true benefits are. If you are completely unsure of the amount the client is responsible for, consider charging a $30 copay until you do know (which sometimes means waiting until the payment and EOB have been received), then adjust as needed. Inform clients that you will adjust their account whenever necessary as soon as you notice any discrepancy. But I do not recommend refunding anything until you get complete payment from the insurance, and then give a refund or credit if necessary.

The Mental Health Parity Act is supposed to go into effect towards the end of 2009 which will require a client's mental health and substance abuse benefit coverage to be the same as their medical coverage. There are some exceptions to the law, but most plans will begin implementing the parity on January 1, 2010. This may make obtaining benefit quotes easier and more accurate because the mental health and substance abuse benefits should be the same as the medical benefits in most cases. Unfortunately, I have read that managed care may increase, because the law will allow mental healthcare to continue to be managed (meaning preauthorization needed, medical necessity determination, etc.). Insurance companies will likely find ways to save money, and managing the care can be one way for them to do that. They may also pick and choose which disorders are covered and which are not. Deductibles might also increase or there may be two deductibles, one for physical and one for mental. Time will tell how this will all pan out, but we can only hope things will actually improve for the mental health side of things.

ADDITIONAL ADVICE ON INSURANCE BENEFIT CALLS

Make sure insurance benefit calls are complete. When checking mental health outpatient insurance coverage, also make sure you check for total number of sessions allowed per year. If the number is limited, or they have had, or are having, other mental health or addictions services in addition to your sessions, you will need to keep track and be careful. I have seen some plans combine benefits, so it is possible to ask the insurance if they can do this. For example, if you have a client that has 30 sessions per year and appears to be reaching the end of those quite quickly, you can ask the insurance if another area of the benefits package can be transferred to outpatient mental health benefits. So, it is possible they would transfer something like what would be allowed for partial hospitalization to be allowed for outpatient sessions. This is rare, but it is worth asking, especially if the client has no source of payment once the insurance is exhausted, and has been doing well with just the outpatient sessions. Have the insurance give suggestions on what can be done. Have them bring it to a supervisor or clinical director for review if needed.

Always get the name of the insurance representative when you call. Document the time, date, name of representative, and what they quoted when you called. Always instruct clients to do the same. If there is some sort of denial, you will have a better chance of fighting it if you have specific documentation backing you up.

Of course, there are billing services that also check benefits and obtain pre-certifications when necessary. This may be an option for you. Just make sure you completely research the organization before you give them such a key role within your practice.

INSTRUCT CLIENTS TO GIVE YOU "NEW INSURANCE CARD" INFORMATION

Make sure clients know that they must bring in any new insurance cards they receive. We have often run into situations where clients received new cards but did not inform us. Frequently, on new cards there are new ID numbers, and other new information on the front and back of the card. If you do not have this new information, it will likely result in a denial of claims.

Make sure your clients know they have to inform you of any upcoming insurance changes, because then you will either have to get a new benefit quote or make some other type of plans for the case. Benefit quotes should be obtained at least one time per year (it is usually at the beginning of the calendar year when changes occur).

BEWARE OF THE "ZERO COPAY" CLIENT!

When insurance clients say they have "no copay" it always makes me nervous. This is because they are not going to expect to pay anything, but as many of you know, that is actually a rare situation with insurance cases. Frequently we find that they do have a mental health copay, or specialist copay. We also frequently find that they have a co-insurance amount or a deductible they are responsible for. So, you are going to want to check everything before assuming "no copay" and not charging anything to the client. If you are really seeing that the client is not responsible for anything out of pocket, then submit the insurance bills as soon as possible to make sure this is actually the case. You are going to want to make sure the client actually has 100% coverage and that you get paid the amount you are entitled to. Sometimes the processing of the bills is the only way you can be guaranteed of that.

COLLECT UPFRONT

With all of your self-pay, superbill, and copay/deductible clients, make sure they clearly understand the agreed-upon rate per session as well as all copay amounts. Also make sure that they know payment is due at the beginning of each session. You can even say it like it will benefit them to keep their account up-to-date by not racking up huge amounts and being surprised later with how much has added up. It is better for clients to pay as they go, than to end up with huge amounts all at once that may be difficult to pay. If the client's best interest is being considered in the conversation, then she will appreciate that more than just a statement such as "I need such-and-such amount now". Along these lines, it is also better for your clients if you are getting paid because then you can stay in business and keep helping them!

If there is a client who owes a significant amount of money and she comes to yet another session completely empty-handed, consider sending her back home to get payment. I would not do any additional "free" services for her (there are some exceptions to doing this as I am sure you all know). If the client does not have the full amount due but partial payment, then take the partial payment, because it is better than nothing. It is much more difficult to retrieve payment from a client who is long gone than from a client who is sitting in front of you. Once that client leaves your office you may never speak with her again, so needless to say you may not see any additional payment once she is gone. Accounts sometimes need to go into "collections". This is rare but it does happen unfortunately. If she has forgotten her payment and has <u>no</u> balance from previous sessions, consider doing the session and then kindly have her either send the payment to your office right when she returns home, or drop it off at your office later in the day or week. The idea here is for you to receive the payment balance *before* the next session. Another method that seems to help is being able to accept major credit cards (if you can afford doing this---shop around for the best deal). When there is a valid card on file it is easier to charge the amount the client owes, after informing the client. You may even want to keep a valid credit card on file, for all of your insurance clients, so that it is easier to charge the card for owed amounts. In addition, at the time of this writing, I have in our Statement of Understanding (SOU) form that there will be a $50 charge for all returned checks and declined credit card charges. My point is that we always make everything very clear to all clients, and they sign all the forms.

If you are feeling stuck with a large bill and the client is not responding to your notices, you can try a few methods. One can be helpful if money truly is the issue. You can offer a payment plan where the client pays a certain amount per month, in order to pay down the balance. Another method might help if money is not the issue. You can ask the client if she was dissatisfied with the services. This usually gets clients talking one way or another. If she was dissatisfied, it will usually get her voicing her opinion. You can then let her know she has been heard, but also that she still is required to pay the bill. Sometimes, lowering the fee a bit can help in these types of situations. On the other hand, if she was not dissatisfied with the services, this question can also get her talking because she will want to make sure it is known that dissatisfaction is not the reason for the unpaid bill. You can then obtain the true reason and go from there. One other option is to ask the client open-ended questions that put the ball into her court. Such a question might be: 'So, what would you like to do to resolve this problem?". This gives her a chance to come up with her own solution for her outstanding bill.

ALWAYS KNOW WHAT THE CLIENT OWES

Have client copay amounts easily accessible. I would recommend writing the client's copay, co-insurance, and deductible amounts on the inside cover of the file folder. Also write in all the contracted rates for all expected services. Know all of your contracts and what you are allowed to charge (and charge for) at the time of service. In addition, have a calculator always available for all percentage copays and such. This way you will always know what the client owes at the time of service.

USE INVOICES

In my practice, if we find a client owes a balance, we bill immediately, as that has been shown to get the most results. Waiting to bill has a higher chance of resulting in non payment by the client. With insurance clients, we inform them of how much they owe and that their insurance is requiring the amount to be paid to us, which really is true, *especially* if that amount was applied to their deductible! But, also if they owe a copay or co-insurance amount, it is required by their insurance that they pay that exact amount to us. If they owe for a no-show or a bounced check, we will state that on the invoice along with "per the signed cancellation policy" or "per the signed returned check policy". You get the drift. Detailed, itemized invoices get sent to the client regularly until payment is made. I have seen that the majority of bills do get paid, when we are constantly in communication with the client. The client has to know that this bill is not going to go away. Kindly give that message to the client.

Another method that can help is to use someone else as the "bad guy". If you work for a practice, you can easily use the owner or billing person as the "bad guy", by saying "so and so is going to need to see some payment here next to this date of service". If you are on your own but someone helps you with your billing, accounting, or business aspects of your practice, use that person as your "bad guy". You can say it very nicely, but firmly. So, you can figure out your plan and who your "bad guy" will be. You can also use your "bad guy" to help in sensitive situations surrounding client no-shows.

I also have on our SOU "There is no guarantee of insurance coverage and you are responsible for payment if the insurance does not cover your treatment". We make sure clients fully understand this and then they sign the form.

It is important to always get the following information from the client (and responsible party) on your "new client information" form: full formal name, home address, phone numbers, and e-mail addresses. If they are getting informed of their outstanding bill via mail, phone *and* e-mail, then they are more likely to pay their bill and much sooner. It is similar to negative reinforcement- if they pay their bill the annoying letters, e-mails, and phone calls will go away! In addition, you are not going to want to get stuck with an outstanding bill and no valid contact information for the client or responsible party.

Make sure all client communications and invoices look official and professional. All spelling will need to be completely accurate. You may also want to input extra wording in later invoices, such as "Payment is severely overdue… Prompt payment will prevent this account from being transferred to collections". If there has been a decrease in rate such as an insurance fee reduction, for the client, show that on the invoice. Clients love to see that they got a discount, or that a fee was waived. So you can list it such as: "Initial Evaluation Fee $130, Decreased Insurance Contracted Rate $90, Total Amount Applied to Client's Deductible $90, Copay Paid $20, Total Amount Now Due $70". Be sure to include after the total "Your insurance is requiring you to pay the practice this amount". If you are giving a client a break with the payment for whatever reason, then put that on the invoice as well, such as: "Initial Evaluation Rate $130, Decreased to $90 as Courtesy to Client". This will remind them of your gesture and might get you paid more quickly.

DEAL WITH DECLINED PAYMENTS

In situations where there has been a returned check or declined credit card charge, you have every right to require a different form of payment, for the current charge as well as future charges. If they have a very good excuse for what happened and have an excellent track record of having no problems with payments to you, then consider taking the same form of payment again. But, if that is not the case, feel free to require another form of payment for their current and future bills. Be particularly careful of taking checks or credit card charges (ones where you bill later online) from clients that have a history of payment and collection problems, or are in debt. I have also found in my practice that I have to be careful taking checks from clients with gambling problems because there seems to be an increased chance that the checks will be returned. If you do decide to take a check or credit card payment from a client like this, deposit it or bill immediately in order to catch any issues as soon as possible. If any issues come up, contact the client immediately, and I would say "cash only" for present and future payments.

DEAL WITH INSURANCE PAYMENT ISSUES

Do not be afraid involve clients if there are issues with insurance payments. After all, it is *their* insurance and I think they really need to know. You have already provided the courtesy of billing insurance for them and many times taking a lowered rate on top of that. You will always need to involve clients if there are problems such as Coordination of Benefits issues, Pre-existing Clauses, or eligibility issues which are holding up payments. In these types of cases, clients have to get involved and answer all the questions the insurance has for them. But there are other situations as well, such as things that appear incorrect, and non-payment when payment was expected. I have found that insurance companies frequently make mistakes, so it would be wise to have clients contact their insurance if there seems to be a problem. We usually word it something like "Looks like you will have to contact your insurance to straighten out a 'Coordination of Benefits' issue, in order to avoid being billed by us". This usually gets clients on the phone immediately.

ADDITIONAL INSURANCE AND GENERAL BILLING ADVICE

It is important to make sure all of your bills are very clear with no errors. For example, a major insurer I am contracted with has a computer scanning all bills submitted by providers. If there is anything incorrect or unclear, it will not pay and will come back with a message such as "no record of membership". So take some time and double-check to make sure everything is 100% legible and accurate before submitting. This will save you a significant amount of time and you will get paid faster.

Bill insurance and credit cards, and deposit all client checks, as soon as possible. When you do this you will see a potential problem much more quickly than if you wait and bill or deposit later. The sooner you find out about problems the better. If you find you need to bill a client, the sooner the better. It is known that the longer the time between the service date and then the billing date, the more likely the person will not pay. So, send those bills out quickly! Later on, when you become more established and you are not seeing so many new clients, you can try billing and depositing less often, in order to save some time. You will still come across some issues, but much less often as your established clients and their payment sources will become more predictable to you in general.

There is one exception to "bill insurance as soon as possible". That exception is when you find that a client has an unmet annual deductible and you also know that he or she may not pay. When you are in business for a while, you will begin to know which clients might not be willing or able to pay. Therefore, if you find an unmet deductible, and there is questionable ability or motivation for the client to pay, then consider waiting to bill the insurance until you either think the client has met (or come close to meeting) the deductible, or the client has paid you for the services (due to the deductible). You will most likely be better off if you wait a while to bill, in this type of situation. However, there is a word of caution on waiting too long to bill, and that is mentioned in the following paragraph.

As frequently as possible, go back over your ledgers and make sure you have gotten paid for all billed sessions. There are some companies that will either reduce the amount paid or not pay anything at all if your bill arrives too late after the service date. I had one managed care company tell me that they were not going to pay for a service because the bill came in too late. When I told them that the bill was initially submitted back within the same month as the service date and this was a re-submission, it did not work. They told me "we did not receive it". So basically I was out of luck because *they* lost it or did not process it the first time around! I could have gone through the appeal process but it was not worth my time considering the way they were responding to my phone call. I now avoid working with this particular company whenever possible, but I just wanted to warn that this may happen to you as well, if you do not stay on top of your ledgers. EAP companies seem to be much more forgiving and flexible with situations like this, especially if you are a good provider for them and ask them for re-consideration respectfully, adding that it will not happen again.

If it has been about a month and a half since you have submitted an EAP bill and you still have not gotten paid, then contact the billing department of the EAP. Make sure they received your invoice, and if they have, ask when you will receive payment. Again, make sure to always speak in a respectful tone with all EAP workers. They have a way of talking with each other frequently, and you may not like what the billing person may say to the referral counselors if you are not coming across as professional. Your relationship with any EAP worker will probably affect the amount of referrals you get. A positive relationship usually equals more referrals.

If it has been over a month since you have submitted an insurance bill and you have not gotten paid, you can contact the claims department to inquire. You may also consider resubmitting your claim instead.

Do you think an insurance claim was processed in error? There are a few things you can do. You can try contacting the insurance claims department to inquire (have all the client information plus the claim number on hand). Something else that seems to work well most of the time is to re-send the claim for "reprocessing". So, with that situation you would copy the claim again (or re-write it) and at the top and bottom of the form write "NEEDS REPROCESSING" and highlight those with a highlighter. I also add a sticky note to the top stating that the claim needs re-processing and the reason why. It is important to flag as "needs re-processing" otherwise it will come back as "duplicate billing" if it has been processed already.

Not sure which client name to bill under? If you are seeing a family or couple and are not sure which name to bill under, if there is one individual that has better benefits (you are in-network, there is a lower deductible or deductible is met for the year, etc.), then consider billing under that person's name if it is okay with the family. Also, if you are seeing a family or couple and the person you are billing under is about to run out of benefits for the year, then consider starting to bill under another covered family member in order to continue their treatment. Of course, the identified client will also need to have a covered diagnosis.

Keep in mind that V-Code diagnoses are not usually covered by insurance. Therefore, refrain from placing a V-Code diagnosis anywhere on an insurance bill. EAPs, on the other hand, usually honor V-Codes with no problem, but you may want to double-check before submitting an EAP bill with just a V-Code on it.

As far as Axis 2 diagnoses go, I do not believe I have ever seen an insurance company cover them (especially if it is not combined with an Axis 1 diagnosis). Therefore, I recommend leaving any Axis 2 diagnoses off of all insurance bills. Now, there are situations where a managed care company may need to know about an Axis 2 diagnosis in order to justify a lengthy treatment. In a case like that, you may want to inform the case manager verbally of this secondary diagnosis. You may even want to write it on the treatment plan as "Axis 2 traits". Placing the actual Axis 2 diagnosis code on a treatment plan as the secondary diagnosis is also an option. I would just refrain from placing an Axis 2 diagnosis on any insurance billing form.

If you have a claim that gets denied due to diagnosis, but you know there is an additional one, ask the insurance if your bill can be reprocessed under the other diagnosis.

Lately, we have run into issues with "serious" versus "non-serious" diagnoses. Unfortunately, some insurance plans are giving less coverage for "non-serious" diagnoses (usually adjustment disorders and such). So, my advice is to diagnose it exactly as you see it, even if it is a more chronic diagnosis. You can also always update your diagnosis later on as well. Long gone are the days of giving a more mild diagnosis in order to protect the client from a more serious permanent label.

SOME ADDITIONAL TIPS ON NEGOTIATING RATES

We have all been there, you have someone on the line that needs counseling, does not have insurance and is asking for sliding scale. If the caller say things such as "I am having trouble paying my electric bill" then you will know it is truly is a sliding scale case. If you desire to take this case and drop your fee, ask him first what he could possibly pay for weekly sessions, which will probably go to every 2 weeks later on. If what he says is considerably less than your absolute bottom, then I recommend telling him what your absolute bottom would be. This is the only type of situation where you would tell callers what your bottom would be if I were you. I would also add that there are only a few slots in my practice where I could allow this rate. In addition, the client would have to be told that once he got back on track as far as his financial situation goes, the rate would have to go up. So do not have that initial agreed-upon rate be permanent, by any means. Remember, when you get a new client, you might be seeing him for years! Are you going to want to take such a low rate years from now? I don't think so.

There are other uninsured individuals who truly need a lowered rate as well, but they can pay closer to your regular rate. When you have one of these people on the line, start with telling him that you might be able to be somewhat flexible with your rate given his situation. Then tell him what your regular rate is. See what the reaction is. If he says there is no way he could pay that, then try lowering it gradually until you come to a rate that you both can agree on (again this would need to be seen as a temporary rate that could change in the future).

If there are some "potentials" that ended the call shortly after you informed them of your rate, I would call them back a day or two later to see if they have any other questions or concerns. If they still seem hesitant but do not come out and tell you it is your rate (which some will not), then ask them right out "Is it my rate there is a concern about?". Then you may get into the negotiation process at that point which is good.

There will be some others who <u>do</u> have the means to pay your full rate, but do not want to pay that much. You know what I am talking about. They have a nicer car than you, live in an upscale neighborhood, and dine and shop at places you cannot. You will have to decide, with these types, whether or not you will drop your fee. If you do, I suggest you do not decrease it by much. If your fee is reasonable already, compared to other local therapists, then I would not drop it at all for these folks if I were you. They probably will not find a much better deal, and if they do more power to them if the rate was their main concern in choosing their therapist.

I would not recommend decreasing the rate for any of your in-network insurance clients. The reasons are that most insurance contracts already decrease your rate considerably, and you are also doing the insurance billing for the client and managing all of that, along with collecting copays. I think that is quite enough! I think it is against most insurance policies to waive any of the portion the client is responsible for anyway. If you have a superbill client (will be submitting her own insurance billing), who has legitimate concerns about the rate and having to pay that upfront, you can drop your fee just a little if needed, pending knowing what the insurance will be reimbursing her. Because if you find that she is later receiving back a good part of what she paid you for services, then she is probably doing just fine and your full rate will probably be alright for her to pay for future sessions.

As mentioned earlier, some therapists use a sliding scale rule of charging $10 per every 10k in the annual household income. So, if the income is 60k, the cost of a session would be $60. Of course there will probably have to be a bottom or minimum you would take, but this can give some type of structure or rule of thumb on what sliding scale fee to charge a client.

Whatever you do with your fees, just make sure the client is in full understanding of any agreement and how things work in your practice. Have them sign your SOU fully spelling everything out, including fees. In addition, do not drop your fee lower than what you would be fully comfortable with for a particular case.

BULK PAYMENTS CAN BE WIN-WIN

Collecting bulk payments can be a good option. Having some self-pay clients pay in bulk, for a discount, works well for us. Some clients go for this because they can get discounted rates. Remember to remind the client, though, that this only works for you if it is paid in bulk upfront, and with all other situations it will have to be your regular rate. So for example, if your regular rate is $130, perhaps you would accept something like a bulk rate of $400 for 4 sessions that is paid to you upfront. You get all of your money much sooner, it is easier for you to manage, and then the client gets a discount for it.

Monthly payments may work well for certain clients. You might set up monthly payments with clients that are self-pay and need a lot of time with you. So you can set it up where they are allowed a certain number of contacts with you every month for a certain fee. Think about the amount that you could do this for. Let them know that you will not be available in the middle of the night and also will be taking vacations, so all of that will need to be considered. You will also need to inform them that the rate may change as you go. Also collect the entire monthly fee towards the beginning of the month, to make sure you receive all the payment for the services. Setting up monthly payments can simplify things for everyone and can meet your needs as well as the client's.

PAYMENT PLANS ARE NOT ALWAYS A GOOD OPTION

Spreading out required payments over several months, called a "payment plan", is not usually a fruitful option from my experience, unless it is a last resort to collect a balance amount. I would not recommend setting up payment plans for new clients, as this has not usually worked very well for us. The problem is that anytime you have a client who is having trouble with his bills (therefore needing a payment plan), and then he is done with his treatment with you, he is likely to skip out on the last few payments of his payment plan. So, he has already gotten what he needed from you and he has financial problems on top of that. It just does not seem like a great mixture to me, and has not proven to be good for us in general. You may, however, want to set up a payment plan for someone who is found to owe a balance later on in therapy. I am talking about the situations such as insurance not paying, or something like that. If a client in this type of situation asks for a payment plan, I would be in favor of that, as long as it was not going to drag on too long, and the payments would be scheduled and sizable enough.

ALWAYS BE HELPFUL TO YOUR CLIENTS

It is known that, in private practice, being helpful to your clients can help you get paid by them, and in a timely manner. In my experience, clients are less likely to skip out on their payments if they feel they have been helped and that the professional truly cared about them. Now, there are exceptions to the rule, such as client bankruptcy, but it definitely helps in the "payment arena" to have given it your all.

It would also seem that clients who feel they need you would be more likely to pay. Therefore, providing and offering highly necessary services to clients and their family members will also help you get paid by them.

APPOINTMENT-SETTING ADVICE

When making appointments, make sure you give the client the appointment time and date along with the day of the week. Give the client enough time to write it all down and then repeat it all again to make sure. When making appointments while in-person, always write the next appointment on one of your cards and give it to the client. Write the appointment date, time, and day of the week on the back of your card. Make sure clients have your cards in all places they might need them (in their appointment books, in their cars, and at their homes and offices). I have one counselor who has her clients program her number into their cell phones so they will always have it and can easily call when needed. This helps decrease no-show/no-call issues as well as late-cancellations. It also would be a good idea to inform clients of where they can find your contact information if they have lost it. For us, we can say that our contact information is on our website, in some phonebooks, in online listings, as well as listed with their insurance or EAP plans (if they were referred). So, let them know where they can easily find your information again if it is lost or they need it quickly.

LOOK AT MISSED APPOINTMENTS DIFFERENTLY

Change "missed appointment" time into marketing time! When you have a no-show or late-cancelation (like all of us have), in addition to charging for it per your cancellation policy, consider spending the free time focused on marketing your practice. Do this instead of dwelling on anything negative. You can spend the time figuring out how to get more new clients as well as activities related to brining your previous clients back in. You might even get an interesting phone call or e-mail during the time you would have been in session. You never know! So when a client is missing her appointment, change negative energy into positive energy and see what comes!

Chapter Five:

Attracting Your Ideal Client

Maybe you would like to attract a certain type of clientele to fill your caseload and have been unable to do so? Of course, working diligently on many of the previous methods and suggestions mentioned should help you meet this goal. This chapter gives some additional words of advice on how to attract your ideal client.

DETERMINE WHO YOUR "IDEAL CLIENT" IS

You might not be quite sure what your "ideal client" looks like. If this is the case, I suggest doing some soul-searching to figure this out. There is a good chance there are certain types of cases you enjoy working with more than others. This is important to identify for yourself and your contentment with your practice. What types of cases seem to fill you up, and which ones seem to deplete you? Which cases tend to make you look forward to sessions, and which seem to make you dread them? Many of you will have a clear feeling or picture here, however there will be some of you that may need to take a bit of time to figure this out for yourself. Once you do, it can benefit you in many ways. The most important way is that it will contribute to your happiness in your work. It will also assist you in writing a professional profile on yourself that will portray your specialties and interests, which will attract your ideal client. Clients may also be able to sense whether you are truly excited to work with them or not, so it is a win-win situation if you know what your ideal clients look like and then they are attracted to you.

GETTING "QUALITY" REFERRALS

Perhaps you would like to learn how to receive more of a certain type of referral, such as non-managed care or higher fee? There are plenty of self-pay clients out there and making yourself stand out will definitely help attract them, many times at your full fee. In my practice, at this point all of us are certified hypnotists in addition to our primary licenses. This has done very well for us in our area, because it is difficult to find a mental health professional who is also a hypnotist. There certainly are not many on managed care lists. So in that way, we certainly stand out in the crowd for clients looking for some hypnosis with their psychotherapy. Therefore these clients are more likely to bypass some or all of their insurance coverage to see us. So think about what additional training you might find interesting and would enjoy doing. Some interesting certifications that I have come across are in the following list. The good news is that none of them seem to be extremely difficult to achieve, yet they serve the purpose of conveying a niche or communicating a specialty:

- Certified Hypnotist (C.H.)
- Emotional Freedom Techniques Certification (EFT-CC)

- Distance Credentialed Counselor (DCC)
- Certified 12-step Consultant (CTC)
- Substance Abuse Subtle Screening Inventory (SASSI) Certification
- Certified Anger Resolution Therapist (CART)
- Stress Management Counselor-Certified (SMC-C)
- Certified Bereavement Facilitator

Whatever your interest is, fully research any possibilities and choose the training that you feel the best about and are able to do. This will make you stand out in the crowd to your ideal clients and their referral sources. Make sure you place this on all your marketing materials and word it such as "Certified Anger Resolution Therapist", and if you can place the certification letters behind your name that will work well (just make sure to explain all of your credentials so that potential clients can see them clearly and quickly, and understand what they are). So, if someone needs anger management, and you are a CART, they will likely call you first.

On your marketing materials, you can also list major trainings you have attended. Include wordings such as "ICASA/ICADV Certificate: Trained by the Illinois Coalition Against Sexual Assault & the Illinois Coalition Against Domestic Violence". It does not have to be a formal certification to include it as something important. Doing this increases your credentials and also gives a clearer picture of your professional interests.

You may also choose to join various associations, such as one for Cognitive Behavioral Therapists, to show that it is one of your methods and you keep up on all the recent news about it. CBT is one method or theory that is frequently sought out by potential clients as well as referral sources. So taking something a step further by joining an association, or showing you have had additional related training, will make you stand out.

Having some unique specialties or interests will help. For example our "Holistic Approaches to Well-being" has generated many referrals. I am simply a practitioner member of a holistic health association and have taken an interest in learning new research along with natural remedies. It is my approach to look at the whole person as well as their life and everything around them, in addition to spirituality and energy. This is how I see all cases and it has done well for me and the counselors in my practice. It also draws the clients in. It is certainly not the usual approach clients will likely get from someone perhaps in their managed care provider network.

So, being aware of trends, filling current needs, and making yourself look different than the average counselor will be important. One of the frustrations we hear from clients is that they cannot find a specialized therapist in their managed-care network. So, set yourself apart and demonstrate your true value in the marketplace through specialization. Many people that are in the market for healthcare value specialization.

WHAT IS YOUR IDEAL CLIENT LOOKING FOR?

Ask yourself what your ideal client might be seeking. Know the answers to this question, and make sure all of your marketing materials will be attractive to your potential ideal clients. What are they looking for and what would they like to see? If you want to work with grief/loss, perhaps your ideal client would like to see that you belong to a professional association of grief counselors, and that you have written an article on grief that you have posted on your site. This will be quite attractive to this type of clientele, and none of it terribly time-consuming or expensive.

Another example situation might be where the potential client is looking for someone who has been through a similar problem, and she feels it would be necessary for the counselor to have that type of personal insight and understanding. For example, a client who needs assistance coping with physical illness might search for a counselor who has been through a severe illness herself. So on this counselor's marketing materials, she may want to mention that her approach to helping clients cope with physical illness comes from dealing with her own past illness. This counselor will definitely stand out in this client's eyes with this information on her marketing materials. There is a unique understanding here that only someone with these types of experiences can provide, and this can be extremely important for a client like this.

WHERE WOULD YOUR IDEAL CLIENT COME FROM?

Ask yourself where your ideal clients may come from. Might it be from the phone book? Might they come from an EAP plan (an employee or family member of an employee)? Maybe they will come from a certain type of internet website? Or maybe your ideal client attends divorce support groups in the suburbs? Perhaps they will be referred by a specific insurance company? Wherever your ideal client may be, or may be looking, you are going to want to have a presence there somehow, and make sure everything there is complete and looks professional. For example, if they might come from a specific insurance company, make sure that company's list is completely accurate as far as how and where you are listed. As I mentioned earlier, it would surprise you to know how many times I found my provider information to be incomplete or inaccurate. These lists are what potential clients, as well as referral sources, are viewing.

BE AWARE OF TRENDS

Watch the news and read your local papers to look for trends! This can spark ideas on current needs in your area and how to fill them. For example, after watching and reading my news, I see opportunities for professionals trained in career-oriented counseling, grief/loss, marital therapy, financial counseling, suicide prevention, insomnia relief, and more.

WORK WITH EAPS

Contracting or working with some EAPs can also give you a referral base of clients who can eventually be self-pay or have insurance coverage for ongoing services. (See Chapter One for more on EAPs).

Keep in mind that if you are not the right therapy provider for a client, which may be determined after her EAP assessment, it is usually fine to refer out to another more suitable provider for the treatment piece. So, do not feel like you have to take every EAP case as a long-term therapy case. Just explain to the client that you feel that another therapist would be a better fit for her actual treatment, include the reason(s), and then make the linkage to the treatment provider.

ANOTHER WORD ON SELF-PAY CLIENTS

Often we get clients that are not sure they want their insurance billed for psychological treatment. This could be a legitimate concern as we really do not know what the insurance will do with their confidential information. There may also be a treatment plan or reviews necessary, so there may be additional concern with that. Clients also need to be told that, in the very least, a psychiatric diagnosis will have to be submitted to their insurance for any coverage to be released. This diagnosis could remain in their permanent record. So, if the client is teetering back and forth about whether or not to use insurance, explain all of this clearly and then he may choose not to use insurance. Then you have a self-pay client, at least initially (note: he may change his mind later).

If you have a client that is looking for something specific only, such as hypnosis, life coaching, or career counseling, it is probable that his insurance will not cover it anyway, so there you go! If you are offering services such as sports psychology, career-oriented counseling, or anger management (for courts), the insurance will only pay if there is a covered psychiatric diagnosis that needs treatment. So you will have to explain that to these clients and also that a psych diagnosis will be submitted and will then be on their insurance record. Some will chose not to have it submitted and will rather self-pay.

I also know that marital and family treatment is not always covered by insurance (particularly HMOs). So, if someone calls asking for couples counseling and she has a very limited HMO that you are not in-network for, let her know that she might not have the coverage anyway. Have her call you back if it is determined that her insurance does not cover this, because they might as well see *you* for their couples counseling then, right?

Some are predicting that if universal coverage gets passed (or if government gets more involved), marriage and family therapy will not be covered. They are also saying that mental health, if it even gets covered at all, will be even more scrutinized for "medical necessity" and "evidence-based treatment" than ever before. They think that people are not going to want to pay taxes on something that is for "personal growth" only. This all may be true, but it might turn out just fine for everyone reading this book, because now you all have the ability to exist without relying on insurance cases alone!

DON'T FRET IF YOU'RE NOT IN-NET!

If you are not in-network for a potential client's health insurance, try not to let that be the end of the call. Ask if he has a PPO plan or another type of plan with possible out-of-network benefits. Because if he does, there will likely be some coverage for him to see you (and sometimes it is not much different than the in-network benefits, especially when you factor in contracted rates compared to Usual and Customary out-of-network rates, which can be much higher). So, you can offer to give him a receipt for services that he can submit to insurance for re-imbursement. This is usually called a superbill receipt. (See Chapter Three for more information under the section "Use the Superbill Receipt"). In my practice, we like using these, as opposed to submitting to out-of-network plans, because we get paid upfront this way and we do not usually have to deal directly with all the insurance issues that seem to frequently arise. This does not mean you will not get pulled in to help in some situations, but it is usually much easier and more lucrative this way. There are some therapists who continue to bill out-of-network plans because there are some benefits to doing so, such as Usual and Customary PPO rates being quite nice, and clients also usually appreciate the billing service. We have found, though, that many clients will go the superbill or self-pay route just because they want to see a specific person, either because they have the specialty or technique that is needed, they have a desired office location, they came highly recommended, or simply because they felt a connection with the counselor and therefore put that before any payment issues.

There are some clients or patients, however, that simply are not going to be able afford to go the out-of-network route even if they really want to see you and you have negotiated down to your very lowest amount, or even offered to bill insurance for them. Unfortunately, those sometimes have to be referred on to someone else, but always say "call us again if your situation changes", because you never know what can happen in the future, or who they might refer later on. Always keep a good reputation within the community by being helpful, courteous, competent, and open to new referrals.

Some clients will choose to bypass their insurance altogether. You will find that some people will forgo managed-care, or HMO, reimbursement. So they will self pay for services that are of high value because they can be of higher quality, offer real privacy, offer more control in decision-making (such as length, frequency, location and amount of sessions, or methods used), and are truly customized for their individual needs. You can tell callers exactly this, and still show respect for their insurance carrier at the same time. Leave the client to make the decision, and hopefully it will be an educated one. Remember not to jump straight into offering sliding scale to these folks. Wait to see what their financial situation is first, and then you may decide to offer it if absolutely necessary. You can always try contacting them again in the future to follow-up and further discuss, if you have not heard from them in a while.

MAKE SURE THEY KNOW YOU TAKE CASH!

It is important that you make sure you include statements such as "private pay" or "cash/checks accepted", as well as "sliding scale fees available (if necessary)", on your marketing materials. You will want to make sure that non-covered clients know they can see you. As I said previously, we have had clients ask us if we take cash! Ummm, YES we take cash! We have also had clients feeling reluctant to speak to us because they did not have insurance. Well, we had to explain that it is just fine as we <u>do</u> take cash, checks, and credit/debit cards. In addition, we have told clients that we can be very creative with setting up their treatment and payments depending on various circumstances when needed. Some of these have turned out to be exceptional long term clients for us.

SEEK ORGANIZATIONS AND GUILDS THAT LINK PEOPLE TO MENTAL HEALTH AND WELLNESS PRACTITIONERS

As mentioned earlier, there are some new and unique organizations that are creating ways for people to access providers and services that may not be covered by (or involve) their insurance. This avenue can therefore be a way to obtain more self-pay clientele. A few of these organizations are contacting employers to provide a membership card for employees. This card would entitle them to discounted services from provider members. There is no insurance to deal with, and no one to approve or deny sessions. Instead, providers agree to offer their services at a discount to members, and the clients pay upfront. From what I have seen, there is sometimes a fee to become a provider member, however this usually includes a listing in their directories which is an added bonus. So, asking around and searching for "guilds", as well as topics such as "alternative health care provider lists" and "health savings cards", may bring you to these types of opportunities.

DRESS TO ATTRACT THE TYPE OF CLIENT YOU WANT

Think about the type of clients you want to attract and how they might dress while coming to sessions. If you want to attract adults that are upper class or business professionals, you might usually want to wear business suits, dress pants or dresses while conducting sessions. These types of clients might be slightly uncomfortable if you are always wearing jeans or something more casual. On the other hand, if you want to attract children, adolescents or more casual (or perhaps blue collar) adults, then wearing a business suit or dress may make it difficult for your ideal clients to connect with you. But if you are usually in jeans, casual pants, or a very casual dress, then it may help you to connect with these clients. If your caseload is a mixture of all types of clients and you want to keep it like that, then I suggest you wear casual pants or casual dresses/skirts during most of your sessions, so you fall somewhere in between and will be able to connect well with all clients.

OFFICE SPACE THAT ATTRACTS YOUR IDEAL CLIENT

Your office space can attract your ideal client and keep them coming back. Therefore, make sure your office always looks inviting because you never know who could be looking in. You will want them to get a positive feeling of what it might feel like having a counseling session in your office. If you want to attract children, then make the office inviting to them. Having toys, small scale furniture for them, colorful décor, and children's activities all will help. If you want to attract more adult upscale or business-type clientele, then you might want to make the office look more upscale or business–like, and you may want your offices to be located near upscale residential or corporate areas. If you would like to attract the teenage client, then having "cool" things in the office will help, such as certain games, décor or magazines, because if it is fun or "cool" for them there, then teens are more likely to return for services. If you want more hypnosis clients, then make sure you have the appropriate furniture for them to be the most comfortable. If your desire is to work with more handicapped clients, then of course you will have to make certain your space is 100% handicapped accessible. Working with larger-sized clients will require you to have various sizes and shapes of furniture. If your office is small, there are ways to create optical illusions to make it seem more spacious. Get some help in making it feel more cozy if it seems too big. Just make sure the office, and the contents, accommodates and makes comfortable the type of clientele you want to attract and keep.

MAKE SURE YOUR AVAILABLE TIMES AND DAYS MEET THE NEEDS OF YOUR IDEAL CLIENT

Having days and times available that will be convenient for you and your clients is crucial. I have found that a mixture of some daytime, evening and weekend hours works quite well when building a practice. Also make sure the times are tolerable for you because you will not last long if the times you can use the office are not the times you want to work or have a lot of energy. It just will not work in the long run and clients may sense this as well.

TAKE CREDIT CARDS

Accepting major credit cards will most likely attract more self-pay and superbill clients and it might be easier for them to pay for additional services as well. It will also help for any bulk payment situations. (See Chapter One under the "Accept Major Credit Cards" section for more on credit cards).

A WORD ON SPECIALTIES

If you have a specialty where you are highly trained and skilled, but you do not particularly like doing the work, shift the training and knowledge a bit to something you do like. For example, a therapist might be trained in alcohol abuse counseling but may not like doing that specific type of work. She could leverage that skill by working with related topics or populations. For example, she could add to her marketing materials that she works with family members of alcoholics, or codependency, or that she does evaluations only. She could also make a shift to a general "addictions" specialty, which may include issues such as smoking and habit cessation, internet addiction, and so forth. So you can use what you have learned from having previous specialties, and shift it a bit towards the particular issues or populations you would like working with. It will be better for your practice in the long run if you enjoy the work you are doing.

OFFER SPECIAL SERVICES FOR THOSE WHO LIVE FAR

Reaching out to populations that live far can add to your income as you can gain more "ideal" clients as well as increase your "income streams" this way. For example, a beginning hypnotherapist may want to offer longer sessions to those who live far away from her office. Also, someone who specializes in grief counseling may want to market to farther away areas and offer telephone sessions to attract more grief/loss cases. These far-away places might be rural, underserved areas within your state. The possibilities are endless if you think about it.

Chapter Six

Keep Them Coming Back

Now that you know how to bring in the referrals and also "make the sale", you will need to have ways to keep your clients coming back for more. This chapter will go over various tips that I have found helpful in order to keep clients coming back. Like I had mentioned earlier, in my practice we have a high percentage of clients who return for more services after their initial sessions.

BE RELIABLE

It is important to keep your appointments and be on time. You will not be able to keep re-scheduling or changing session days or times on your clients. Being continuously late in beginning your sessions is also not going to work. You will need to respect their time as well as understand their psychological need to see you as reliable.

GIVE EXPECTED AMOUNTS OF TIME WITH EACH CLIENT

It is necessary to give clients the amount of time they expect to have with you. If you happen to be late starting a session, then you will have to stay a bit later with that session, or offer telephone or online contact to make up for the lost time. You may also choose to have the next session be a bit longer if that is more feasible for both of you. I am not saying to go over the amount of time clients expect to get. Just make sure they do not feel cheated and are getting the amount of time they expect to receive from you.

GIVE AN "I OWE YOU" WHEN NEEDED

When you have to late-cancel an appointment, give the client an "I owe you" in return. So, if you are in a situation where you have to cancel a scheduled appointment and it is late notice, then make sure the client knows you owe her a late-cancel for "free" in exchange. This can keep the relationship respectful and positive.

OFFER A PHONE SESSION IF THERE IS A LATE-CANCELLATION

Consider offering a phone session if you get a late-cancellation because the client cannot come in, especially if the client will be paying your full fee anyway. But do phone sessions only if you feel comfortable, because anything other than just collecting your full cancellation fee will be a favor to the client.

CONSIDER BEING FLEXIBLE WITH THE FIRST LATE-CANCELLATION

If there is a late-cancellation and it is the client's first offense with a decent excuse, consider waiving or at least decreasing your missed appointment fee. If you waive or decrease the fee, let the client know that you are doing it for this time only, due to the situation, and then thank him for at least calling ahead. This gesture will show consideration for him, but it also protects you (sets an understanding of a limit), and shows that your time matters as well. If this type of situation happens one time with one of your long-term reliable clients, I would recommend waiving the fee. With these types of clients you do not need to set so many firm limits because they already know and follow the rules. You will want to show appreciation for this and keep them as a client.

Some therapists do not charge for a late-cancellation if the client can come in at another time during that week. Whatever policy you create, just make sure you feel comfortable with it as well as any other agreements you make.

Again, along these lines, if you have a client that has special needs, such as a physical condition, and she may need a special cancellation policy, then consider doing so. For example, I might need to change my cancellation policy for a client who has a chronic physical illness. If I see that this client usually knows four hours prior to our appointment whether or not she can make it, then I may set up a "four hour cancellation policy" for her. So, do this when needed, when it is also feasible for you. You may keep a good client this way.

LOOK OFFICIAL

Looking official and established will help you keep your clients! Therefore, anything you can possibly do towards this goal will be beneficial. Make sure you have a name plate on your door (including credentials). Have your business cards and brochures in your waiting area. Your license is required to be displayed, so I highly recommend framing a color copy of it, along with any other certifications and diplomas. As mentioned earlier, displaying or making available any articles you have written, or have been involved with, will also help you look official, credible, and established.

BE RESPONSIVE

Show that you are responsive to clients by calling or e-mailing clients back as soon as you possibly can. Also make sure they know when you are "off", as well as how long it might usually take for you to respond, so that they do not have high expectations and will not be disappointed later on.

REQUEST THAT THE EAP RE-OPEN A CASE

If you saw a client for counseling under an EAP in the past and the client is contacting you again, see if the EAP can open a new case and authorize another block of sessions. Usually EAPs are willing to do this if some time has passed or it is a "new" issue for the client. The client would also need to have the same EAP coverage of course. So, if the client's main coverage with you would be under the EAP, and they would have trouble self-paying, consider this option.

HAVE A WAITING AREA

A comfortable area for clients to wait can benefit you and your clients in many ways. First, with a nice waiting area you can encourage clients to come early to all sessions. If they come early and are sitting in a comfortable room reading health educational materials, viewing your articles, listening to relaxing music, enjoying your interesting décor, and perhaps drinking chamomile tea, don't you think they will feel like they are getting more from your services? I know they will. It is nurturing for them and for you. It is nurturing for you because it is much better for your schedule if clients come a bit early to sessions. You will also be less likely to have to begin sessions with clients that are feeling rushed and stressed from their day and the drive there (many of you know what I am talking about!). You can encourage your clients to think of their time at your office as a break from daily stressors and a place to self-nurture. In addition, if you are running late with your appointments and clients have to wait, you will not feel as rushed or stressed when you know they are waiting in a comfortable place.

MORE ON THE SUBJECT OF OFFICE

In my opinion, all you really need is an office that is nicely decorated, clean, and in a good location in a decent building. Make sure your offices are comfortable, safe, relaxing, and professional. Make sure the items that are "in view" in your office are pleasing to the eye, are clean, look good together, and are relatively comfortable. Having soothing colors and pictures will work well, and use lamps with soft lighting. Have someone you know who is skilled at decorating help you out if you cannot do it yourself. Play relaxing music in your waiting room and have healing books or magazines for clients to read while they are waiting. Some type of white noise machine will be important, to protect confidentiality. Make sure your office smells nice, but do not overdo it with any heavy perfumes, deodorants, or cleaners. Just make sure your office is clean, and if needed use a very mild or natural freshener, that does not overpower as some of your clients will be sensitive to this and have allergies. Also, do not smoke cigarettes before sessions as some clients will not return for services if there is a strong cigarette odor.

BE TRUSTWORTHY

If you tell a client you are going to do something, then do it as soon as possible in order to gain trust. For example, if you do not know much about a subject they are sharing about, and you say that you are going to do some research on it, do the research before the next appointment (or at least before the time you say you will have done it). This will show that they can trust in you, you care about their problems, and you will do what you can to help them.

Making sure clients know exactly what they are responsible for as far as payment goes is always a good idea. Keep the lines of communication open. In addition, if you bill credit and debit cards, it is important for clients to know exactly how much is to be billed and for what services.

Taking session notes will usually be fine. Just keep the communication open. Let clients know you are only writing down some things *they* are saying, and you just want to make sure nothing is missed. Also, inform them that they can feel free to see the notes you are writing. If they still have difficulty with your note-taking after discussing it, I would recommend exploring that because it might be diagnostic, such as a feeling of paranoia.

GIVE CLIENTS SOMETHING TO LOOK FORWARD TO

You might tell clients that in the next session you will have something for them, such as a hand-out or book, in order to give them something to look forward to. You may something such as "In the next few sessions I would like to focus on such and such and really help you to come to a resolution for yourself. What do you think about that?". Give them something they can look forward to receiving from you.

Creating hand-outs can be beneficial for you and your clients. You can take some popular topics like sleep problems and create handouts such as "sleep tips". Give these to all of your clients that have insomnia issues. You can also create custom hand-outs for certain clients, such as cognitive-behavioral worksheets tailored to a specific client. They will probably be touched by this and will be much more likely do their "home therapy" assignments as well! Include your letterhead on all custom handouts, as clients may refer to them at a later date and also may give them to others. Creating handouts also shows that you have a high interest in your work and in serving clients. It also shows that you want to make sure you help them in every possible way.

PORTRAY A THIRST FOR KNOWLEDGE

As we all know, there is always more information to learn in every field. Between the new discoveries and the latest techniques uncovered, there is always something else to gain. Let clients know that you are always looking for sources of new information. If there is a way to educate yourself about a specific client's issues, let them know you will be doing that. Put yourself in your client's shoes. For example, imagine you are a client who sees a counselor due to needing assistance with a recent diagnosis of a chronic illness. Say that the counselor tells you that she will be attending a professional education seminar entitled "Assisting Clients in Coping with Physical Illness". Imagine how you would feel as that client. I would imagine you would feel that your counselor is excited to learn more about the issues that you need assistance with and that you will be coming back in order to gain from the additional knowledge the counselor will have after the seminar.

COMMUNICATE THAT YOU ARE HAPPY TO SEE THEM

Make sure you greet all clients with a smile and communicate that you are happy to see them. This might not seem very crucial to some, but trust me it is. It is important for them to know you are glad to have them as clients and like working with them. Do not assume they know this.

INCLUDE POSITIVE STATEMENTS OR ACTIVITIES

I have found in my work that doing or saying something positive towards the end of sessions works well. You can always come up with some sort of positive theme in a person or in one's life. For example, say a woman comes in discussing a devastating illness she has. After having her vent and express herself, and validating her feelings, I would pick out something positive at the end such as "Well it looks like, though all this, you do have what sounds like a truly wonderful husband, and that's a gift you've been given, something you can hold onto to get you through". So this does give her something to "get her through" and think about. It is very positive and gives her a positive association with therapy. She will likely want to come back for more. Also I suggest doing something fun or interesting in every session. For example, maybe have a new joke to tell a teenaged client at the beginning of each session, or perhaps work with angel cards at the end of each session for your more spiritual clients.   Maybe you decide to include discussing therapy gains periodically.   Let your creative side come out and come up with things your ideal clients would appreciate.   Whatever you decide, just make sure they leave each session on a positive note.

PAY CLOSE ATTENTION TO WHAT CLIENTS SAY THEY NEED OR WANT FROM SERVICES

In order to make sure you know what your clients are needing, you are going to want to gently ask the following open-ended questions to all your regular clients sometime around the first appointment:

"What do you feel you need to receive from coming here?"
"What things do you hope to gain from me?"
"What do you hope happens after coming to sessions?"

I believe that clients are experts in themselves, and given the right conditions and guidance, they will know intuitively and will choose what feels right for them.   We cannot tell clients what to do, especially if we have never been in their exact situation.   It needs to come from them, and you will lose clients if you keep pushing something that is not "clicking" with them.   Now, there are situations where you will need to remind the client of his goals and educate him as to the avenues through which he can reach those goals. Nonetheless, it is important to provide caring, empathic, and individualized attention to all of your clients.

GIVE RECOMMENDATIONS

One piece of your services that clients are paying for is to hear what you recommend for them. This does not mean telling clients what to do, but it does mean recommending or suggesting certain activities, services, books, articles, groups, and so on. Also, feel free to recommend further counseling, or at least follow-up services, with you if you feel it would be beneficial in any way. Be sure to document all of your recommendations in their files even if they refuse to follow through on them.

PROVIDE INSIGHTS

Let clients know if you see any possible connections in what they are saying. Of course, in traditional psychotherapy you are going to want to have clients come to as many insights on their own as possible, and you can suggest activities that can increase their insight and intuition. But, sometimes you are going to want to assist a bit more in the process, letting clients know of possible connections you are seeing. I recommend wording it such as "I have a hunch that the dreams you are having are related to such and such from the past". Now, I would not word it as "The dreams you are having are from such and such from the past", because you do not really know for sure. This is not an exact science, and perhaps the dreams are a result of several different factors (some of which can be unknown to you, such as a medical condition).

LET CLIENTS KNOW THAT YOU THINK ABOUT THEM OUTSIDE OF SESSIONS

Make sure clients know you think about them at times between appointments. If something positive or inspiring reminded you of your client, be sure to tell her that you thought of her and during what situation. If something else got you thinking about her specific difficulties, let her know that as well. Clients like to hear that we think about them sometimes and care about their needs. This is a great way to communicate that, connect with them, and keep them coming back.

AVOID OVERLOADING A TRAUMATIZED OR GRIEF-STRICKEN CLIENT

Many clients come to us traumatized or grief-stricken in some way, and it is important not to overload these types of clients. I think you can identify this type of case, and you will probably know it quite quickly. With these clients, expect to listen most of the time and talk only to give supportive words. If you talk too much in any kind of judgmental way, or ask a lot of loaded questions to this type of client, she might leave feeling even more overwhelmed and confused than when she came in. At the end of session, you might give some simple advice or education. But mainly you want to thank her for sharing, convey that you understand what she is saying, tell her that you think you can help, and give the message that you would like to begin a counseling relationship with her. Most times these clients simply want someone to understand what they are going though and they want to connect with someone. This is not a time to introduce psychodynamic insights to clients. It is a time to meet them way down where they are, and fully understand and connect with them.

LET ALL OF YOUR POSITIVE QUALITIES SHINE THOUGH

As a professional, it is important to come across as non-judgmental, understanding, resourceful, assertive, and intelligent. Let those sides of your personality shine through. Humor, at times, can also be quite beneficial! Be yourself and also make sure you show the positive qualities that you possess. It will be more fun for you and will help keep them coming back for more!

Chapter Seven

Support, Validation, and Encouragement

I know most of the difficulties you might be going through during your practice-building experience. I have been there myself and have been through it with the professionals I have assisted, as they were building their practices. This chapter contains various supportive words of advice that have helped me and the other professionals I have worked with while practice-building.

GETTING SUPPORT, VALIDATION, AND ENCOURAGEMENT

It is imperative to get support, validation, and encouragement for *yourself*. You will no doubt have your own needs during your practice-building experience. I suggest that you first reach out to other business owners for support. Reaching out to other professionals who work in a little different area of specialization, or different location, can work well. Then you can support each other without feeling like you are competing with one another. You can give referrals back and forth as well. Joining a social or networking group with other therapists may also help, either online or in person. For example, you may want to try a local "Meetup Group". In my area, we have one for social workers as well as one for mental health professionals. Surely, I could find many more if I looked into it, such as one for business owners as well as healing professionals. Please note that it is best for you to be able to trust the people you are sharing with in these groups and also receive something in return. If not, then take the benefits of it (e.g., referrals or resources) and leave the rest. A word of caution: when you start doing well, your competitors will find ways to take your good ideas or methods and may try to copy them. I guess if that happens, you know you've made it!

CONSIDER GETTING YOUR OWN MENTOR, CONSULTANT, ADVISOR, OR COUNSELOR

Confidential professional assistance can help tremendously in many ways, for yourself and your practice. It can provide much-needed support, guidance, and encouragement. It can also increase insight into yourself which can significantly help your work with clients. Even if it is something such as seeing a spiritual advisor, it can help greatly. If you fill yourself up in these ways, clients will sense this, therefore it is a win-win situation for all involved. So, I urge you to check in with yourself regularly to see what your needs are in this realm. Remember that most services related to helping your practice are tax deductible!

SELF-NURTURING WILL BE NECESSARY

A counselor who worked in my practice used the term "self-nurturing" quite regularly and I think it's brilliant! So, check in with yourself regularly to make sure you are doing well. If you are feeling irritable, tired, or stressed spend some time figuring out what your needs are for that day or week. Have ways to get your mind off of the little details of your practice and onto the bigger pictures, including the things that really matter most in your life. Some activities that help me self-nurture are: getting back to nature, reading, spirituality, hobbies, movies, family time, connecting with others, eating right, and getting enough sleep. I also take Sundays completely off from any private practice work. So, taking large blocks of time away from your phone, e-mail, and paperwork will be needed. Make sure clients know when you are "off" and what the emergency procedures are for when you are not available. You will need this time to "fill up" in order to be productive again and have the energy to serve your clients well. Also, taking a break and spending time in new surroundings can spur creative ideas for your practice.

Only in quiet waters things mirror themselves undistorted. Only in a quiet mind is adequate perception of the world.

~ Hans Margolius

ATTEND A DAY-LONG CEU SEMINAR

Choose a CEU seminar on a topic that is exactly what you have been wanting to learn about and sign up for it. This can be tremendous for your self-nurturing. During this day, you can connect with other professionals, ask questions to the speaker, learn useful information that can be used in your practice, and confirm that what you are doing are indeed good methods. I have found these types of gatherings to be quite energizing and nurturing. You can also find time to rest and relax during these types of days. You deserve it!

KNOW ALL OF THE PROFESSIONAL RESOURCES FOR YOURSELF

Check into all of the resources that are available to you, such as legal consultation resources through either your malpractice insurance company, or perhaps through membership with a major professional association. Take advantage of free clinical case consultation from your clients' EAP and managed care companies. There are also free online billing programs available to clinicians (the only charge is to the insurance companies!). So, there will almost always be someone or something to help you with any issues that may arise for you and your business.

MAYBE YOU JUST NEED A PUSH?

Perhaps you already know several effective low cost marketing methods and have good ideas, but you need someone or something to motivate you to work on them. In this sounds like you, consider getting a business coach, consultant, or mentor to "prod" you. You may also consider a supportive relationship with another business owner who also wants to build, and you can make sure you both are doing what you need to do in order to expand your businesses. Perhaps having a checklist or "to do" list that you are required to complete every day would do the trick? Whatever it is, I know that you would have excellent advice for others, so what advice would you have for yourself? Take that advice and go with it!

ARE YOU HAVING MOTIVATION ISSUES?

If you are having trouble motivating yourself to complete the activities in this book, ask yourself some important questions. First, ask yourself "Am I completely sure I like direct client service?" If your answer is a solid "yes" then that is half the battle because that is the ground work here. If you are not sure about the answer, then be completely honest with yourself. Would a different area of work be better suited for you? Or perhaps you enjoy administration and supervision more. In that case maybe you should consider hiring others to do the direct service work in your practice, and you perform the other duties. Perhaps you like client work but dislike doing long-term therapy? Maybe you discover that you no longer want to attract a certain type of client. Or perhaps you discover that you need some additional training in some areas in order to feel more confident selling yourself or getting clients to return for more services. Whatever it is, there is almost always an answer and a solution. The fact that you attained your professional education and also are reading this book indicates that you are at least somewhat interested in your field, so do some soul-searching to find the answers for yourself and re-invigorate the energy of your practice.

DO NOT GET "DOWN" ON YOURSELF!

It is important not to get "down" on yourself just because you are seeing other professionals doing well. The only differences between you and them might be that they have been around longer, maybe have a few more credentials, and know how to get their information out to others who are looking for their services. I remember when I first started my own practice. It took many weeks to even get a phone call. The first was from a potential client who was referred by a lower-paying EAP that I had a contract with. The client came for one session and then did not return for more services. Then I had a call from a woman who saw one of my online listings. We talked for a while on the phone, then she said she'd think about it and would call me. Well, she never called. What I am trying to say is that I went from that situation to my current situation where I am getting multiple referrals on most business days. I am the same person now as I was with no clients. I have just been in business longer, have a few more credentials, know how to get my information out to people that need or want my services, and know what to say to them when they contact me. This can happen to you as well. So, do not, I repeat, do not measure your self-worth on how many clients you have scheduled in a given week. I completely understand how it can feel (as I have been there myself), but as you know it is completely irrational to think that way. Look at other successful professionals as inspiration, and if you are feeling jealous, then make your goals the same as what you see in those professionals.

DO NOT LET OTHERS BRING YOU DOWN

We all know that some people frequently say negative things. If you listened to other people all the time and did not listen to your own intuition, you would be in trouble! So, tune in to yourself and if you feel strongly and positively about something, by all means do it! This reminds me of a situation that occurred back when I was choosing my business name. I decided to use my own name for my corporation name. Then we told everyone about it and someone laughed and said sarcastically "Ha! How original?!" At first I thought, "Oh maybe I should name it something else?" But then I remembered why I felt this was the best thing to do. Some of the main reasons I used my name for the corporation were because there would already be some name recognition benefits, it was the easiest way due to existing contracts I already had, it sounded professional, and "G" would come up on alphabetical lists somewhat well. So, I made a good decision considering all of these reasons, plus it felt right to me and my situation.

Great spirits have always encountered violent opposition from mediocre minds.

~ Albert Einstein

ONE MORE BIT OF SUPPORT

A mentor once told me "you cannot be everything to everyone". I will always remember that statement as it has helped me tremendously. Trying to be everything to everyone will be too stressful, unnecessary, and the services will be too general for the client. So there are some clients or cases that just are not "my cup of tea" but they are perfect for another counselor, and vice-versa. In addition, there will continue to be clients who do not "click" with me for whatever reason, and that is perfectly fine. It does not mean I am not a good counselor, especially because of all the other clients that <u>have</u> "clicked" with me. My point is, do not beat yourself up for any of this. Just get back up and do the best you can with your current cases and work towards drawing in more clients and positive things into your practice. Positive self-talk and some cognitive-behavioral techniques for yourself may help wonders!

To serve is beautiful, but only if it is done with joy and a whole heart.

~ Pearl S. Buck

Chapter Eight

Additional Words of Advice for Your Journey

This chapter gives various additional tips that I have gained through the years and found to be quite helpful. Therefore, anything additional that I felt needed to be said in this book in order to help you is collected here in this chapter.

LOOK AT ALL OF YOUR OBSTACLES IN A PRODUCTIVE WAY

As with any business and any professional, there will be problems. Look at them as challenges you can overcome and hurdles you can jump over. Also look at them in a "what can we learn from this" attitude. When you cannot do anything else but learn from something, take the lesson and move on.

ORGANIZATION AND FOCUS ARE NECESSARY

If you are not naturally an organized person, you will need to find systems or people to help with this. Without organization and focus, things will fall through the cracks, with ethical and financial consequences. If you are having trouble focusing on details of your practice, you will need to figure out what is at the bottom of that, as the root cause. Then use your problem solving skills to resolve it. If you have too much going on in your life and at home, you will need to prioritize, let some things go, and set aside time where you can focus 100%. This is a difficult decision I know, but it will need to happen. Multi-tasking does not really work in the long run.

THE IMPORTANCE OF ETIQUETTE

Thank everyone who helps you. If you are given a lead, a phone number, free advice, or anything that can make your life easier, make sure you give them a "thank you" message in return. This will communicate to them that you received the information, it was helpful, and you really appreciate it. This will motivate them to help you even more in the future and, who knows, maybe even send a referral your way!

BE PROFESSIONAL AT ALL TIMES

It is important to always sound professional, competent, knowledgeable and kind to every potential client or referral source. This includes e-mails. Always follow e-mail etiquette, as well as correct grammar! It is one of my "pet-peeves" when professionals do not use proper grammar in their correspondence or there are mistakes. There is no reason for it, and it will come across as sloppy and unprofessional, and frankly unintelligent (sorry!). Correct grammar gives readers confidence that you know what you are talking about. How you come across can make or break a potential referral. This also includes your voice mail greeting. Very important! Again, make sure it sounds inviting and professional. Have others listen to it to see if they would feel comfortable leaving a message for an appointment at your establishment. Welcome their honest feedback. Remember, whoever you are talking to today can refer someone tomorrow, so look at every interaction as marketing, even if it is one on one.

ALWAYS SEE YOUR AGE AS AN ASSET

Let me just say that your age can always be a "positive" for clients. Think about this. Young people can be seen as more energetic, more "in touch" with what is going on in society, and are seen as having the most "cutting edge" knowledge and techniques. Older people are seen as having more wisdom and experience, they tend to have more of a calming effect on others, and are more relaxed and comfortable in general. So, always use your age (no matter what it is) to your advantage! If clients say you look too young to help them, you may have to prove to them that you can. If you feel they might think you are too much older, you may have to show you are in touch with today's society, and then show all the wisdom of life you can offer as well. But you never really know what the client is expecting and it does not seem to matter much in the grand scheme of things in my opinion. I have done some of my best work with clients that were my parents' age. In addition, I remember having a client who was age 24 and I was 33. She sat down with me and said "I thought doctors were supposed to be old... I don't know if I can do this". Then she did not return for many more services. So, even though I was almost ten years her senior, it was not enough. I would not have expected this from a client her age. My point is that you just never know what they might get "hung up" on, so just try to keep the communication lines open and do your best.

Another interesting story about age is when I was working as an EAP intake counselor, I was speaking to a caller who was requesting an appointment with an older counselor. She said "I don't want a 24-year-old social worker. I want someone like you... someone like you can help me". Well, little did she know I <u>was</u> a 24-year-old social worker! My point here is that I <u>could</u> help her and she knew that. My age would not have mattered in getting her the assistance she needed. She may have tried to place age concerns in between getting help if she was seeing me in-person and could see how young I was. When obviously I could be of assistance and she was aware of that.

A WORD ON GENDER-NEUTRAL NAMES

If you have a name that can be used for either a male or female, it would be a good idea to convey your gender in some way on your written advertising. Using your full name or a picture may help. Certain wording or messages can also aid in conveying gender. This way, clients who are looking for your specific gender will not pass you up.

ONLINE COUNSELING IS ONE OF THE NEWEST INTERVENTIONS

As many of you know, most therapists now have yet another avenue in which to provide services, which is through the internet. Now, for some client populations, this is a highly needed form of counseling. For example, it is extremely helpful for people who are home-bound, hearing impaired, physically impaired, those that need a particular specialty that is only offered by far-away therapists, and those that have unpredictable travel schedules. I am grateful that there is a way to connect with these clients through online counseling.

If you are interested in this type of work, there is a market for it. I suggest that you search the internet for some websites that you could join as a professional member in order to provide online services via their sites. These types of organizations provide secure servers and other necessities for online counseling. I recommend that you sign up with as many online counseling sites as you can, in order to get a more complete schedule, as you so wish. Read and participate in all of the training they have available (there are specific details you will need to know), and understand all of the policies and how everything works in each site. You may also be able to see some of these folks in your office if they are somewhat close in location, or at least conduct some sessions over the phone. Also consider combining online, in-office, or phone counseling in order to get to know a client a bit easier. You may also wish to use online counseling as follow-up after traditional therapy. Online counseling could be considered another "income stream" for your practice, which is always positive. If you are serious about this mode of therapy, it might be smart to invest in a web cam for your computer (I do not think they cost much), so you can actually see your online clients who also have video capability.

As you get more experienced in this form of counseling, you may consider setting up your own online counseling site. However, it may take a considerable about of time and knowledge, as well as support from a computer specialist, in order to set it up properly.

Be sure to inform your online and telephone clients of all the pros and cons of doing these types of sessions, compared to being in-person. One concern is that some information might be missed or misunderstood, and another concern might be about confidentiality.

BE AWARE OF YOUR OWN INTERNET PRESENCE

To monitor your online presence, periodically search the internet for your name as well as your practice name. You might be surprised what one can find out there! Hopefully it is all positive, but if not, or you want something to be kept private, you might have to do a little work on that. Be careful of anything you input into any site because it may be able to be viewed by everyone. For example, I placed some reviews of gluten free restaurants as well as made a comment about some gluten free cookies online. Then when searching my name later on, those comments always came up. Luckily they all sounded positive and were not really too personal. If they were negative or too personal, I would have to work on getting them removed. So, think before you post anything! This applies to social networking sites as well. Although those profiles and postings are considered more private and usually only in view of your "friends" that you invite, you never know if something could get out somewhere, and you are going to want to remain careful with anything on the internet. Manage any negative reviews or items by looking through or contacting the internet site to see how you can do that.

DEAL WITH COMPLAINTS IN A PROFESSIONAL MANNER

I, of course, am not a legal professional, but I have had to deal with some complaints like all practice owners, and therefore have some suggestions. If a client is complaining to you about your service or practice, let the client know that he has been heard and that you care about what he has to say. I would not admit fault in most cases because, from my experience, the complaints in this business typically are not based in fact and do not come from any professional experience. Rather, they seem to usually be based on feelings or reactions to something. If you are continuing with the client, then I would further discuss the real issues he is having surrounding the complaint, give some of the rationale for what happened, and if appropriate, would inform him of how you would be doing things a bit differently in the future given the new information. If you will not be continuing with the client and you have him on the phone, I would just briefly communicate to him that he has been heard and that you care about what he has to say. I would then thank him for his input, offer up a list of possible therapists for continued treatment, and discontinue communication with him. If you deal with complaints in these ways, you can decrease the likelihood of some sort of formal complaint and you may also prevent your reputation from being tarnished.

Our greatest glory is not in never falling but in rising every time we fall.

~ Confucius

BE HONEST

Being honest could come back to you in many positive ways. For example, let's say you find that a previous client has a small credit with your practice due to an insurance payment amount that was unexpected. Contact the client promptly and let her know she has a credit. This can be a great segway into asking her if she would like to come back in for services and use her credit that way. If she is not going to come in anytime soon for more services, let her know you will send her the money. When you send her the check, be sure to include a few of your business cards. When and if this client needs services again in the future, it is highly likely she will contact <u>you</u> due to your honesty and attention to her. In addition, if anyone she knows needs services, it is highly likely she will pass along your card.

BE CAREFUL OF UNSUPPORTIVE EAPS

If you ever get a strong feeling from one of your EAP accounts that they would not support you in the event of a complaint, then end that contract immediately. There are still a few EAPs out there that would rather hang an affiliate counselor out to dry than make themselves look unfavorable in any way (usually to their business contracts). So, stay away from these companies. Hopefully their reputations will eventually catch up to everyone and they will go out of business. But, until that happens to all of the bad seeds out there, always be aware of what is going on and protect yourself in all situations. Your reputation, your sanity, and the future of your practice are far more important than getting a few EAP referrals from these types of companies.

DO NOT LET EAPS TAKE ADVANTAGE OF YOU

Some EAPs may try to take advantage of a situation. For example, if they call you to do something like an on-site task where you would have to keep your schedule clear, then they late-cancel on you, you deserve some compensation. They know this, but they will try to get away with not paying anything, in most cases. So I suggest requesting the full amount you were to receive for the on-site time, due to the late-cancel and the fact that you kept your schedule clear. They will probably "meet you in the middle" and give you half of what you were to get for the on-site time. This is usually the standard way of doing things, from my experience. But go with your gut. If something feels unfair, then something probably is. You are entitled to something on your end. Assertively and professionally address the matter with the EAP.

DO NOT BE AFRAID TO REFER OUT

Are you are feeling that a certain case is "over your head"? If so, then you will probably need to look into doing at least one referral with the case. If you are feeling this way, it is apparent that you cannot be the only support for the client or family. If you feel unqualified for a particular case (even if you can obtain consultation on it), then talk with the client as soon as possible to begin the referral process. Do not be afraid to say that you are recommending a higher level of care to the client. A higher level of care could mean some type of facility program or it can also mean a higher amount of education or expertise in a provider. It is okay to admit this and should be said as early as possible in the treatment process. The client may even respect you more for admitting this and putting his needs before your continued income on his case. Just make sure the linkage to other services or providers is very smooth and seamless for clients, and that they are supported through the process.

For clients who begin to show signs of not being able to afford your services, start looking into other options such as area sliding scale or community services for them. Have this ready, so if there comes a time when they cannot pay, you will be able to quickly give the referrals, resulting in more timely linkage. This will most likely be a better situation for all involved.

BE ABLE AND READY TO SET LIMITS AND BOUNDARIES

In private practice, you will have to set strong limits and boundaries, with your clients and with yourself. If you do not do this with your clients, it will feel like a "free for all" and you will end up getting angry and burned out, trust me. If you do not set limits with yourself, you will feel the same, angry and burned out, because your personal life will be too intertwined with your business life. This will not be good for your health or the health of your practice. It will not be good for your family's wellbeing either. So be sure to set firm boundaries. Again, inform your clients on how to reach you in between their sessions and for what reasons it would be appropriate. Inform them also of when you work and when you are off, including when to expect a return call or e-mail from you. Give them instructions in case of an emergency, and set up automatic e-mail responses for when you will be away from your computer for long periods of time. Also, put basic emergency instructions in your voice mail greeting so you do not feel like you need to constantly check your messages.

Swap vacation coverage with another therapist in your area, so that you do not feel like you need to check in during your time of rest and relaxation. Also, when you are covering for another person, you may get a new case out of the deal which is an added bonus!

HAVE A "NO GUARANTEE" CLAUSE IN YOUR SOU

I have included a sentence in our SOU form that clients sign at the beginning of services. It states "As in all counseling practices, there is no guarantee of a positive outcome". I use this because I do not want any former clients calling asking for a refund (or to waive payment) because they were not "helped". Services were rendered and there was a fee for that. There is no refund unless the client has overpaid.

SEE WHAT YOU ARE ENTITLED TO IF YOU WORK FOR SOMEONE ELSE'S PRACTICE

If you are a professional who works for, or is associated with, a practice, do some research on all you can receive from them. You will want to find out about various items such as case consultation opportunities, as well as your presence on all of their marketing materials. See if they will be providing business cards and if you can set them out in the waiting areas of all the practice offices. See what they can offer as far as professional name plates and such. In addition, if you have an article you have written, see if you can place it in all of their waiting areas as well. You may also ask if you can get paid more after bringing in your own referrals or contracts. If this is not possible, then maybe there is some other type of bonus they can give for bringing in your own clients. I urge you to research all the possibilities for yourself, but also caution you to not be upset if you do not always hear the answer you would like to hear. Remember that practice owners are probably not getting rich off of you (especially if you have just started) and they need to make something in this arrangement on their end as well.

SOME ADVICE ON HIRING OTHERS

Hiring others, adding associates, or using outside services for your practice can eventually make your life much easier. It can also improve the chances of getting more referrals as the referral sources will usually think there is a better chance that client needs will be met by a group practice rather than an individual practice. In addition, having others join your practice can help you feel less "alone". However, if the others you bring in turn out to be the wrong fit for your practice, it can be a nightmare. So, that said, make sure you completely interview any new candidates, as well as potential contracts or outside services that you would like to use in your practice. Check all references. I recommend running everything by all the others involved in your practice first, and having all of them interview and approve the candidates as well. Have the candidates make sure they are fully informed about the type of situation they would be entering with your practice. It is a good idea to give them some time to think about their decisions and have them do whatever research is necessary beforehand. Be very clear and upfront about what your practice can offer them and what it cannot. Everyone you let in will have to sign a detailed contract and follow it. They will also need to have a very clear understanding of everything you will be expecting of them and their positions. It is much better for them to make informed decisions than having to leave in the midst of significant client caseloads. If you decide to use someone for your billing, the same goes here. Do your homework beforehand. Check references and reputations. Stay involved so that if something goes majorly wrong, you can easily just intervene and take the work back.

Do not hire people in efforts to try to save them from bad situations. In the past, I had made some negative decisions because I thought, unconsciously, that I could (and needed to) "save" people from the awful jobs or poor financial situations they were in when they interviewed in my practice. This ended with some negative consequences to me and my practice. So, my advice is do only what is right for you and your situation at that current time, and separate all other possible agendas from that. Trust your gut and intuition. If something or someone does not seem completely right for you and your business, or the timing is off, and you have some reservations, then do not proceed with that person or service.

KEEP COPIES OF EVERYTHING

One reason to keep copies of everything is that it is just good practice and it can protect you in the future if there is some sort of dispute. Another reason is that you will probably use the same information, if not the same forms, in activities such as applying to all the lists you will be on (e.g., insurance and EAP lists). This will save you a great deal of time.

ADDITIONAL ADVICE ON NEW REFERRALS

Always save "new client" messages until you know for sure you have written down the correct contact information. Write down the caller's phone number and name immediately, just in case you accidently delete the message. This has happened to me a few times and it is a terrible feeling. In addition, keep a referral log of everything that has come in as well as how they were referred. Always have a pad of paper with you so you can jot down any messages. Place them in your referral log file so they are kept altogether and in a safe place.

I recommend contacting all new referrals at least three times before assuming they are not interested in an appointment anymore. So, contact them immediately after they have contacted you, then a few days later if there was no luck, and then a few weeks later if still no response. Many times clients lose contact information or they are not completely ready to commit to an appointment yet. There are many reasons, so do not assume you do not have the case after just the first call has failed. Give it more chances and more time, making sure you give your contact information very clearly two times on each call back. I recommend not calling too frequently or too many times though, and also be careful not to sound desperate or negative. Always sound very positive, like you are looking forward to speaking with them and helping in any possible way.

ANTICIPATE AND PREPARE FOR THE SLOWER TIMES IN YOUR PRACTICE

In my area, summer and the holiday season are two time periods when our referrals and client sessions usually slow down. Therefore, since some of the fruits of your marketing may not come for a month or more, prepare for the slower times by stepping up the marketing methods before the slower times begin. So for me, I would have to step it up in the spring for the summer slowdown, and would have to step it up in the fall for the holiday slowdown.

YOU NEVER KNOW WHAT CAN HAPPEN TODAY!

You could get three new referrals today! Believe me, this can happen at any time as this business can be quite unpredictable. I remember when first starting out, just when I was about to say "boy it's slow... I haven't gotten a referral in a long time", that is when the new referrals would pour in. So it can happen at any time, any day. Remember this as it will energize you and create excitement for the future where anything is possible.

Chapter Nine

Final Thoughts

After reading this book, my hope is that you have newly found excitement about the future of your business. No doubt, this is a difficult time, the marketplace today. But, there are also opportunities out there now for hard-working creative professionals to fill current needs, and build their businesses at a low cost. Success takes time, that I know for sure. Be patient, and then each year you are in business, you will likely have to do less and less marketing to achieve the same results. Your practice will likely require continued care and attention in this regard, however, just not as much as the years go on. There may be times when your caseload drops for various reasons (or for no reason at all it seems), so you will probably have to go back and do the methods again. You will soon begin see the fruits of your labor once again, and your caseload will build back up.

Diversifying by developing a large number of referral sources as well as a few different "income streams" increases the chances you can create significant income ongoing, and it can be rewarding in other ways as well. In my practice, we have set up countless referral sources as well as different "income streams", therefore if a few dry up, we will be fine.

Having solid clinical knowledge and skills may be enough for providing quality services. However, it is not enough to get new referrals and attract enough clients to build a practice. Receiving referrals on a continual basis and finding ways to increase income (and the bottom line) are necessary for building and sustaining a successful business. However, this is where many professionals struggle. After reading this book, you should now have "the blueprint" to build and grow your business, and keep it going strong. "The blueprint" is knowledge that graduate school most likely did not teach you.

If you are a gifted counselor with decent credentials, have a nice office and location, are helpful to your clients and genuinely care and connect with them, you will quickly have a thriving practice if you are passionate about your business and follow the methods and advice in this book. In addition, after reading this book, hopefully you find that you are coming up with even more ideas for your practice on your own. That is the way I hope you start thinking about your business. The opportunities and possibilities are endless.

Energy and persistence conquer all things.

~ Benjamin Franklin

Happy Marketing to All of You

Index

Made in the USA
Lexington, KY
10 September 2011